STAN TOLER'S
PRACTICAL GUIDE TO
LEADING CHURCH BOARDS

HOW TO PLAN AND PARTNER FOR
PRODUCTIVE MINISTRY

STAN TOLER

wesleyan
publishing
house

Indianapolis, Indiana

Copyright © 2012 by Stan Toler
Published by Wesleyan Publishing House
Indianapolis, Indiana 46250
Printed in the United States of America
ISBN: 978-0-89827-596-4

Library of Congress Cataloging-in-Publication Data

Toler, Stan.
Stan Toler's practical guide to leading church boards : how to plan and partner
for productive ministry / Stan Toler.
pages cm
ISBN 978-0-89827-596-4
1. Church committees. 2. Church officers. 3. Leadership--Religious aspects--
Christianity. I. Title. II. Title: Practical guide to leading church boards.
BV705.T65 2012
254--dc23
2012036088

To O. A. Garr, III, a dedicated layperson,
a pastor's friend, and one of the finest board members
with whom I've ever served

CONTENTS

PREFACE

Church boards are notoriously difficult to work with for pastors, but they don't have to be that way. While a church board has the potential to be a pastor's biggest headache and stressor, it can also be your biggest ally in ministry. What's the difference between having a board that's a headache and one that's a partner in ministry? Often it has to do with the way the pastor leads the board. That's why I've written this practical guide—to lead you step-by-step through some of the key leadership skills you'll need to lead your church board well.

Leading a church board can be a daunting experience—especially for a new pastor. And even pastors with many years of experience sometimes still struggle with how to lead a church board effectively. The great thing is that no matter what your past experience with church boards is like, you can learn to partner with them for effective ministry in the future. As with all the practical guides in this series, my goal is to give you both the big ideas and the nuts-and-bolts tools you need to lead your church board effectively.

My aim is to walk with you through the frustrations and the breakthrough moments as you learn to partner and plan with your church board for effective ministry. Together we can do it!

STAN TOLER

ACKNOWLEDGEMENTS

Many thanks to the team at Wesleyan Publishing House, especially Don Cady, Craig Bubeck, Kevin Scott, Jeff Ray, Rachael Stevenson, and Lyn Rayn. Thanks also to Ron McClung for valuable editorial assistance. Thank you for helping me elevate this project to a new level.

1

PURPOSE

UNDERSTANDING THE
VALUE OF CHURCH BOARDS

*Pastors must work with boards to achieve
a church's full potential.*

Two board members flinched at the loud crack. They had not
been looking directly at Pastor Don so they did not see him
slam his open hand down on the desk. But those two plus all the
others were riveted on him now as he said, "I am sick and tired
of this constant questioning of every expenditure we make. We're
doing the best we can. Yes, finances are tight. They are nearly
always tight in a growing church."

He paused and realized his outburst had changed the whole
mood of the board. It had been a long time coming. Yet again, a
couple of members—it was always the same ones—had picked
apart the financial report, questioning many expenditures. In
Pastor Don's mind, their questions were a slap at his leadership.

As the financial pressures mounted, he wondered if he was
going to have to lay off a staff member. How else could he find
the extra dollars to make a difference in their tight financial
situation?

And now, how was he going to rescue the board meeting? Every eye was on him. His outburst was so out of character that everyone sat speechless.

Finally, Pastor Don said, "I think we should pray. We need God's help, not only with our financial problems, but with our attitudes about the financial problems."

The Problem with Boards

Pastor Don's predicament is not unusual. All churches face financial pressures. Few are flush with extra money. And worse than the financial stresses are the tensions they can produce on a church board. Most laypersons on boards are involved in their own day-to-day activities with jobs, families, and other interests. They may not have even thought much about the church since the last meeting. Now they're called upon to deal with the church's financial and other kinds of issues. The challenges of working with an elected board have caused some people to become cynical. Some leaders have even questioned the value of boards. Many pastors have thought, "Life would be so much easier if I didn't have to run everything by the board." But church boards serve an important function. Pastors do well to quit dreaming about life without church boards and instead focus on maximizing their effectiveness.

Peter Drucker has written that a strong board is an asset to the nonprofit organization: "You depend on the board, and therefore you can be more effective with a strong board, a committed board, an energetic board, than with a rubber stamp. The rubber stamp will, in the end, not stamp at all when you most need it."[1]

The "Yes" Board

When a governing body simply does whatever the leader proposes without questioning and thinking matters through, it is a weak board. Some pastors are tempted to find ways to handpick their board members, choosing only people who agree with them and do whatever they propose. While every pastor enjoys having people around who agree, it's important that board members think independently of the pastor—whether they end up agreeing or disagreeing on a particular matter. Independent thinking leads to robust discussion and better decisions in the end.

After all, agreeing with the pastor or church staff is not the church board's primary function. It is to provide oversight and to ensure the organization is operating in alignment with its values to achieve its mission—to fulfill the Great Commission however the local church envisions that taking place. And offering and listening to alternative opinions in the context of a healthy discussion will help. However, when the focus of the pastor or board becomes to win an argument or get their own way rather than how best to achieve the mission, problems arise.

The Adversarial Board

Sometimes an adversarial relationship can form between the pastor(s) and the board. Most often, this happens when a pastor or board member digs in his or her heels and refuses to give credence to other perspectives or opinions. They enter meetings with the perspective that their way is the right way and with a determination to not back down. This happens when a pastor or board member enters a meeting with a predisposition to argue. It is usually a sign that either the pastor or board member or both have failed to take the time to listen to each other, even outside the board meetings.

Much is accomplished in the "meeting before the meeting." This is a discussion between the pastor and one or two other key persons. The pastor knows if he or she has the support of these people, his or her proposals will be approved. Without their support, approval is unlikely. These meetings help prepare opinion leaders to influence others. If these meetings never take place, misunderstandings can easily result.

David Allan Hubbard depicted the ideal board as one in which the board members own the organization. By this, he did not mean they "own it as though they were stockholders voting blocks of stock." Rather, "they own it because they care." He said, "They actually own it in partnership because, in a sense, the organization belongs just as much to others."[2]

To have board members with a sense of investment in the church and who desire to see it prosper and fulfill its mission in the best possible way is valuable.

Biblical Qualities for Board Members

When the apostles chose lay leaders in the first church at Jerusalem following the day of Pentecost, they chose seven men who were "known to be full of the Spirit and wisdom" (Acts 6:3). Every church since then has needed laypersons who are full of wisdom and the Holy Spirit. The job descriptions of modern-day board members do not typically include waiting on tables, like those first seven lay leaders. Yet the issues confronting church boards require men and women to be at their best, to use wisdom in dealing with the issues they face.

Faith, Grace, and Power

One of the original seven laypersons chosen in Jerusalem was Stephen, who was "full of faith" and "full of God's grace and power" (Acts 6:5, 8). These are likewise commendable qualities for board members. They serve as advisers and counselors to the pastoral staff, as well as being decision-makers for the local congregation.

Centuries earlier, the wise man said, "Where there is no guidance, a people falls; but in an abundance of counselors there is safety" (Prov. 11:14 RSV). This is one reason boards are so important. They prevent the pastor from shouldering the burdens of the church alone. They provide safety and security. Together they find a better way than any one person would discover on his or her own.

Wisdom

Wisdom is skillful living—the ability to make wise choices and live successfully according to the moral standards of the covenant community. The one who lives skillfully produces things of lasting value to God and the community.

—Allen P. Ross

Wise Counsel

In a similar vein, the wise man said, "Without consultation, plans are frustrated, but with many counselors they succeed" (Prov. 15:22 NASB). Fortunate is the pastor whose board members come together to consult about the issues the church faces. After deliberate consultation, they provide wise counsel to the pastor. They make well-informed decisions that result in success for the church.

The wise man had undoubtedly learned from experience that a person with discernment provides insight into complicated problems. He wrote, "Wisdom is found on the lips of the discerning, but a rod is for the back of him who lacks judgment" (Prov. 10:13).

The pastor is not in a position to punish someone who uses poor judgment. But with a group of wise counselors, the pastor is less likely to be led astray by unwise persons who offer poor counsel.

Wise and discerning board members will listen much, talk sparingly, and come together to make sound decisions.

So a wise pastor looks for men and women to serve on the church board who will not just be agreeable to whatever the pastor proposes, but who will use discernment, sort through the information available to them, and make sensible choices. As the writer said, "The heart of the discerning acquires knowledge; the ears of the wise seek it out" (Prov. 18:15).

The Bible makes it clear that we can have wisdom if we ask for it (James 1:5). Blessed are the pastor and church board who seek his wisdom together.

The Board's Purpose

Ask the chairman of a for-profit corporation about the purpose of its board and you will always get some variation of an answer about minding the corporation's bottom line—whether that be profitability for stakeholders or some other measure. Once there is agreement on how to measure the bottom line, the board can make decisions about staffing and direction that will help the company succeed.

The purpose of a church board is ultimately to mind the "bottom line" of the church—to make sure the church is operating in such a way as to accomplish its mission. But sometimes a church's bottom line is harder to define.

Mind the Bottom Line

In the church, the bottom line sometimes looks different to different people. Even if all board members agree that the church's purpose is to fulfill the Great Commission, the board members still may interpret success differently.

Some may say, "The pastor is doing a great job; look at how many people have come to know Christ as Savior." Someone else may say, "Yes, but are those people being discipled? Are they becoming fully devoted followers of Jesus Christ?" Still others may say, "Our pastor is doing well. The sermons are biblical, relevant, interesting, and worship attendance is climbing." Some may observe, "Yes, but what about the youth ministry? If we aren't reaching and discipling our young people, then what's going to happen to the church in twenty years?"

And on it goes. You may have as many different interpretations of the church's purpose as you have board members. If they find it difficult to agree on the church's purpose, they will struggle to understand the board's purpose.

Remember the Reason for Existence

If you were to ask board members, "What is the reason for the board's existence?" some might say, "We are elected by the congregation to carry out the business of the church." Others may think, "We are here to serve as the spiritual leaders of the church." Someone else might add, "We're here to advise the pastor and assist in making the very best decisions on behalf of the church." Still others may think the board exists to safeguard the doctrinal purity of the church. Some may focus on the physical property and want to be sure the church facilities are properly maintained while others are more concerned with the welfare of the people.

Some churches have two boards. The terminology may vary, but for some it's a board of elders and a board of deacons. Supposedly, the elders oversee the spiritual welfare of the church, while the deacons pursue the physical needs of the church body. Often a third group, the trustees, cares for the buildings and properties owned by the church.

Local churches and their boards have personalities, just as individual people do. So regardless of the particular polity of the church—its method of governance, policies and procedures, and unique practices—the pastor must learn how to work with the church board to define the reason for its existence so that together they can advance the work of the kingdom in that specific parish.

Purpose

In one of George Moore's novels, he tells about Irish peasants during the Great Depression. The government of Ireland put them to work building roads. This worked well for a time because the men were happy to have jobs. But when they discovered the roads led nowhere, they grew listless, began leaning on their shovels, and stopped singing. Moore wrote, "For people to work well and sing there must be a destination."

Fulfill the Board's Purpose

Here are some guidelines to use in helping the board fulfill its purpose.

The Board Has a Responsibility for the Spiritual, Moral, and Social Maturity of the Church Membership. In larger churches, the board may delegate aspects of its work to committees or action teams. For instance, there may be a membership committee that interviews prospective members and sees that they are adequately prepared for the privileges and responsibilities of membership. But the board is ultimately responsible for the church's new members.

The Board Is Concerned with the Buildings and Properties.
While a board of trustees may have the direct responsibility for
the maintenance of the church properties, major decisions about
facilities will still come to the church board for approval.

The Board Serves to Counsel with the Pastor. The board can be
the eyes and ears of the pastor within the congregation. This does not
excuse the pastor from personal contact with parishioners, but a church
board will often have a better sense of the church's history, practices,
customs, and idiosyncrasies. As they share this background, they
enable the pastor to do a better job of ministering to the congregation.

The Board Oversees the Church's Finances. No pastor should
handle the church's finances. A treasurer should be charged with
this responsibility and give regular reports to the church board.
Ideally, the board will work with a budget. Even though a church
might have a finance or budget committee, final decisions about
financial policies and procedures are the purview of the board.

The Board Is Responsible for the Church's Outreach. While
an evangelism committee may be tasked with overseeing the
church's outreach, the board must still
concern itself with reaching the community for Christ. When a church
ceases to care about the spiritual welfare of its community, it has ceased to
have a reason for its existence. To
make disciples in fulfillment of the

Advice

Advice is like snow; the
softer it falls, the longer it
dwells upon and the deeper
it sinks into the mind.

—Samuel Taylor Coleridge

Great Commission means we must first reach people with the
gospel of Christ. Never allow the reaching of attendance goals—
as important as they may be—to substitute for seeing men and
women, boys and girls make decisions to follow Jesus.

The Board Is Responsible for the Church's Discipleship. New believers must be placed in small groups or one-on-one relationships in which they can grow in Christ. We bring them in; then we build them up. We rescue them from certain destruction, but then we must disciple them into fully devoted followers of Jesus Christ. A godly lifestyle, becoming a reproducing Christian, is always our goal for each believer—not just to make the life-transforming decision to follow Christ.

The Board Is Responsible for the Care of the Congregation. Jesus often used the image of sheep and shepherd to describe the relationship of God to his people. The apostles Paul and Peter saw the pastor as a shepherd as well. As the church grows, the congregation may become too large for one shepherd. The board can assist the pastor, through programs of pastoral care, in providing spiritual care and counseling for the members of the congregation.

The Board Oversees the Church's Relationship with the Pastor. Most boards, even if they have a pastoral relations committee, have final say on recommending to the congregation that they renew the pastor's tenure. In churches that are not congregational in polity, the board may make the final decision in this matter. In either case, the board plays a crucial role in the church's relationship with the pastor.

The board can be the pastor's best friend or worst nightmare. An adversarial relationship will only deteriorate further over time. A congenial, collegial relationship will flourish, and together you can accomplish great things as you work for the advancement of the church.

Working with Boards

In a brief but poignant article, H. B. London, Jr. made several practical observations about working effectively with boards.[3]

1. Never begin a meeting without covering it in prayer. Pray for wisdom, patience, and understanding. Pray that you will have the right spirit and that God's Spirit will guide the board meeting from beginning to end.

2. Be in continual, consistent communication with your board in order to sell your vision in less official settings. No board member has authority as an individual. Members only have authority as a group. Yet they are individuals with their own needs, cares, and joys. As you get to know them and invest in them, they will come to trust your leadership.

> **Prayer**
>
> The one concern of the devil is to keep saints from prayer. He fears nothing from prayerless studies, prayerless work, prayerless religion. He laughs at our toil, mocks at our wisdom, but trembles when we pray.
>
> —Samuel Chadwick

3. Be willing to compromise when necessary. You don't have to win every issue. Most proposals can be improved by hearing other ideas. Even if your idea doesn't look exactly like it did when you began, decide where you really must take a stand and where you can make compromises.

4. Stay on topic. So many meetings disintegrate when board members stray off issue. Focus on the big picture. Avoid getting sidetracked down alleys that will dissipate your energy and divert the board's attention.

5. Always be ready to ask, "Is this discussion God-honoring? Are our attitudes Christlike?" A visiting denominational executive, after observing a difficult meeting, told one of its leaders, "Your group needs to decide if it is going to behave in a Christlike manner or continue to be immature in the way members relate to one another." The meeting might well have profited from an interruption that urged the members to pray before proceeding.

6. Treat every member and his or her contribution with respect. If you want people to respect your leadership, you must be prepared to treat them with respect. Respect their history and viewpoint. Respect their time; be prepared; and run an efficient meeting.

7. Make sure each member has sufficient information to make well-informed decisions. Many young pastors present an idea and expect the board to approve it immediately without question. Meanwhile, board members have not had the time to thoroughly process the idea, as the pastor has. Give them time to mull over a proposal before you expect wholehearted approval.

Furthermore, welcome their contributions. You don't have to have all the great ideas. Your board members are intelligent people who make positive contributions in their places of work, study, and community. They will make positive contributions in the church too if you welcome their input.

Compromise

Compromising will help you work together as a team and develop "we-ness" in your relationship. And as you collaborate, you'll discover that giving a little isn't giving up or giving in.

—David and Claudia Arp

Remember it's God's church, not yours; his battle, not yours; his victory, not yours. Go forward!

Results of the Desk-Pounding

Pastor Don and the board, reeling from the shock of his angry pounding of the desk, bowed in prayer. Actually, at the pastor's suggestion, they knelt in prayer. One board member after another asked God for wisdom and direction regarding the church finances. Incredibly, Pastor Don heard someone weeping. When the time of prayer ended, Tim, who had been a board member for years, dabbed at his eyes with his handkerchief and asked for the privilege of speaking.

He confessed that he had been overly critical of the pastor, the church staff, and the handling of the finances. "I realize the bigger problem is my own attitude," he said, and asked the board members to forgive him.

Assurances came from various board members that he was forgiven. Other members spoke encouragingly of their belief that God would help them to face and solve their financial woes.

Pastor Don later told a colleague, "I would never encourage someone to use anger to bring about a board revival, but I think in this case, God used it to shock all of us into facing ourselves and our attitudes."

Action Steps

1. Which of the dysfunctions mentioned do you see in your own church board? How can you go about improving the situation?

2. Develop a list of the purposes of a church board and ask your board members to rank them according to priority. Analyze the results and see how close they come to your priority ranking.

3. Look again at H. B. London, Jr.'s observations about board meetings. How many of the items are you doing well? How many are you doing poorly? How will you improve those areas that are weak?

2

ROLES

DEFINING THE ROLES OF
CHURCH BOARD MEMBERS

*Understanding the board's roles is the
first step to a board's success.*

I'm not going to watch this church decline like the last church I attended," Gene said as he and the pastor sipped their coffee early one morning. "It was heart-breaking watching that church go downhill, making one bad decision after another."

He went on to describe the way his former church had drifted away from the basic teachings of its historical theology. The worship services became formal and routine, devoid of any enthusiasm. The pastor's sermons became little more than benign essays or book reports.

"I feel like my God-given role on the church board is to watch against compromise and decline, to be sure we never drift away from the 'faith of our fathers,' as that other church did," he concluded.

If Pastor Joe had to put Gene's understanding of his role succinctly, it would have been "watchdog." He watched over the doctrine, defended the faith, and guarded against too much change too quickly. While the pastor admired Gene's dedication, he hoped Gene would be able to lift his aspirations beyond watchdog to a more positive role on the board. Always on the defensive, it was difficult for Gene to embrace positive new ideas and programs that could help the church achieve the spiritual vitality he wanted.

Faulty Roles

Pastor Joe is not alone in his concern. Pastors everywhere see board members caught up in typical roles that potentially hinder the life and growth of the church.

Church Bosses

A colleague told me that prior to his first Sunday at a new church, someone warned him, "Watch out for Bruce Smith [not his real name]. He's a church boss."

Not only was Bruce Smith a longtime member of the church, he also served on the church board, as well as other boards in the community and denomination. He certainly was a person of influence.

But when my pastor-friend had the opportunity to observe the dynamics of board meetings in person, he was pleasantly surprised at what he saw. Bruce Smith would often be the first to speak to whatever issue was on the floor. Yet as discussion continued around the table, Smith would sometimes move to do the opposite of his initial statement. Smith was interested in what was best for the church. If other board members had better ideas, he was humble enough to reverse his opinion and pursue a different way.

Because Smith spoke first and because he was a man of strong opinions, some thought of him as a church boss. But the pastor learned Smith could become a powerful friend and ally.

Defenders of the Faith

Other board members, like Gene in the opening story, are defenders of the faith. Preserving the church's doctrine is important, but there's a difference between being a defender and being defensive.

Those who are defensive often have their antenna turned the wrong direction and are quick to assume others are attacking the faith. They may interpret any new idea as a bad one. Once defenders begin to bare their teeth in defense of the faith, they may find it hard to back down and reverse their opinions.

Guardians of the Treasury

Other well-meaning board members may become guardians of the treasury. Such persons are frugal to a fault. Such persons take a commendable trait—a desire for good stewardship—and carry it too far. Instead of discriminating between good and bad expenditures, necessary and wasteful things, they tend to view all expenditures with suspicion. They question everything. Thinking they are providing a real service for the church, they really create a roadblock.

Chief Antagonists

Unfortunate is the pastor who must tolerate board members who have become chief antagonists. Whatever you are for, they are against. It's almost impossible for them to muster up a positive attitude about anything. Their negativity can spread like a cancer. Their poor attitudes can contaminate the entire board and afflict the whole congregation. To overcome the negative effect of a person who looks at life through dark glasses, the pastor will need positive people on the board. In addition to allies, a pastor dealing with a true antagonist needs prayer and a strong positive attitude to overcome the wet blanket this person can throw over an issue.

Class Clowns

Occasionally, you may encounter another role on a church board—the ecclesiastical equivalent to the class clown. To these people, everything is funny. We can appreciate those who find the humor in life situations. A little comic relief helps all of us to lighten up and enjoy life more. But these people have trouble settling down to accomplish serious business. They find it hard to concentrate on meaningful matters, preferring instead to pursue shallow humor, often at the expense of others.

Elders and Overseers

When the apostle Paul left the island of Crete, he had not completed everything he wanted to do. So he left Titus on the island to "straighten out what was left unfinished and appoint elders in every town" (Titus 1:5).

Paul did not simply tell Titus to appoint elders; he gave him specific things to look for when making these appointments. From the original language in which the letter was written, we find two roles these leaders were to fill.

In English, Paul described the ideal person as an "elder" (v. 6) and an "overseer" (v. 7). In Greek, the two words are quite different from one another. The word for elder is *presbuteros* and the word for overseer is *episkopos*.

Elders

What's the difference between these terms? While describing the same leaders, they are defining two different roles. *Presbuteros* means "old man" or "bearded one." If you travel to Eastern countries today, you will find that old men often have beards, and many of them are grey beards.

In Old Testament times, a group of these men served as leaders in a community. They often sat at the gate of the city. When the wise man described the wife of noble character in Proverbs 31, he said, "Her husband is respected at the city gate, where he takes his seat among the elders of the land" (Prov. 31:23). It doesn't mean he spent all his time at the city gate, although that may have been part of his duty. But it means he was one of the leading men of the city. People looked up to him and respected him as a leader among his peers.

When the Jewish people scattered after the destruction of Herod's temple, if there were twelve Jewish men in any city, they were free to form a synagogue. The synagogue always had a leader or governor, and that person was called *presbuteros*.[1] So in these various contexts, the *presbuteros* was a leader. The community recognized him as a person of wisdom and maturity and capable of leading others.

Maturity

A mature faith is homogenized. I'm very impressed with the approach of one church that offers a program called "Growth" one Saturday a month, and laymen have a chance to consider their total lives. One time they talk about investments, for instance. Another morning, they'll discuss ambition or office politics. They're making an attempt to homogenize faith and life, and to me, that's a step toward maturity.

—Fred Smith

Overseers

The other word Paul used in his letter to Titus is the word *episkopos*. This word means to "watch over," "look after," or "care for."[2] While the word *presbuteros*, though it is Greek, seems to have originated from a Hebrew way of talking about their leaders, *episkopos* seems to have come from the way Greeks talked about their leaders. When Greeks overran cities in their conquest of areas and nations, they placed one of their own men in a position of leadership over that area. The word they used to describe that person was *episkopos*, or overseer.

When Paul and others traveled throughout the Mediterranean world establishing churches, they needed leaders, people with wisdom, insight, and maturity. They also needed people who were capable of overseeing others, people with leadership skills. So when Paul wrote to Titus, no one word would cover all he intended to convey. So he called them by both terms. *Presbuteros* would register in the minds of those with Jewish backgrounds, and *episkopos* would resonate with those with Greek backgrounds.

The Character of Leaders

Paul went on to talk about the kind of character and behavior these leaders should have. He said:

An elder must be blameless, the husband of but one wife, a man whose children believe and are not open to the charge of being wild and disobedient. Since an overseer is entrusted with God's work, he must be blameless — not overbearing, not quick-tempered, not given to drunkenness, not violent, not pursuing dishonest gain. Rather he must be hospitable, one who loves what is good, who is self-controlled, upright, holy and disciplined. He must hold firmly to the trustworthy message as it has been taught, so that he can encourage others by sound doctrine and refute those who oppose it. (Titus 1:6–9)

When he called for "blameless" persons, Paul was not insisting on flawless behavior, but rather he wanted Titus to look for people of integrity. He was thinking of people who believed the right things and who practiced what they preached. Titus was to look for men who had their families under control.

He was also looking for disciplined individuals. Harry Truman, thirty-third president of the United States, said, "In reading the lives of great men, I found that the first victory they won was over themselves . . . self-discipline with all of them came first."[3] Paul wanted Titus to find people who were not overbearing, quick-tempered, or violent, and not intemperate in their use of alcohol. Rather they were to be self-controlled, holy, and disciplined.

Stuart Briscoe has described these persons in three concise phrases.[4] An elder should be a "steward who loves God's church." A steward is entrusted with the affairs of another. It is a great honor and privilege to be so entrusted by the Lord.

Stewardship

Dutch politician and theologian Abraham Kuyper said, "There is not a square inch in the whole domain of our human existence over which Christ, who is Sovereign over all, does not cry: 'Mine!'"

Yet Christ calls upon us to be stewards of what he has entrusted to our care.

An elder should be a "student who loves God's Word." How can we lead God's people in a way that is consistent with biblical principles if we do not know God's Word? This is why Paul insisted that the elder "must hold firmly to the trustworthy message as it has been taught, so that he can encourage others by sound doctrine and refute those who oppose it" (Titus 1:9).

An elder should be a "shepherd who loves God's people." When Paul gave final instructions to the elders at Ephesus, he told them, "Keep watch over yourselves and all the flock of which the Holy Spirit has made you overseers. Be shepherds of the church of God, which he bought with his own blood" (Acts 20:28).

Anything else we say about the roles board members take must be set against the backdrop of these biblical principles.

Four Key Roles

When David Hubbard was president of Fuller Theological Seminary, he defined four roles he expected the members of his board of trustees to fulfill: governors, ambassadors, consultants, and sponsors.[5]

Governors

As governors, they sat in meetings and voted. They could vote "yea" or "nay," but in casting their votes, they were governing the institution. Local church board members provide the same function in the congregation. They govern the local church. Their votes determine which direction the church will take. When they govern wisely, the church prospers. If they do not, the church suffers.

The opportunity to govern is the reason many board members agree to serve. Some are motivated by a desire to make a contribution. Others may be more motivated by a desire to control. I have known board members who served because they were afraid of what others might do to the church if it fell into the wrong hands. Whatever the motive, those who serve on the board govern the direction the church will take.

Ambassadors

Board members also take on the role of ambassadors. As Hubbard says, in this role, they are "interpreting the mission of the institution, defending it when it's under pressure, representing it in their constituencies and communities."[6] Especially when the board makes difficult or unpopular decisions, its role is crucial in helping the congregation to understand those decisions. Board members have the opportunity to interpret what the board does to those who do not have all the facts.

Board members may also need to defend the pastor when he or she is

Ambassadors

Jeanne Kirkpatrick, former US ambassador to the United Nations, said, "When the Syrian ambassador acted up, what I really felt like saying to him was, 'Go to your room!'"

May it never be said of our board members—lay or clergy—"You're not acting in a becoming way; go to your room!"

under pressure. They can present a united front along with the pastor in steering a clear course for the congregation. As ambassadors, their influence works both ways: They represent their constituents to the board and represent the board to their constituents.

Consultants

Board members also take on the role of consultants. Laypersons will have skills and experience the pastor does not have. They may be able to provide expertise that would cost a great deal of money if the church had to hire a consultant. A committed layperson, equipped with abilities, talents, and proficiencies, can be invaluable in providing counsel and guidance for the pastor and staff of the church. Such persons derive great satisfaction in knowing they have served God and the church by doing what they were trained and skilled to do.

Sponsors

Finally, Hubbard observed, board members are sponsors. In the case of the seminary he led, he expected board members to give financially to the institution proportionate to their means. He also expected them, in their giving, to assign a high priority to the seminary. In other words, he expected the seminary to be nearly as important to them as their local church. Further, he hoped they would remember the seminary in the final distribution of their wealth, by including it in their estate.

Pastors certainly have the right to expect the members of their local church boards to give generously to the church. In fact, some pastors insist that their board members tithe. If the members will not tithe, the pastors explain, they want members to have enough integrity to resign from the board so that others who have a greater level of commitment may serve.

The Effective Board

Mark O. Wilson, a diligent pastor in northern Wisconsin, has creatively used an acrostic of the word B-O-A-R-D to suggest five things an effective board will do well.[7]

Believe

An effective board will operate by faith rather than fear. It will pray for guidance, which is absolutely essential. Mark says, "When faced with a big challenge, what you do next reveals what you really believe about God."

I couldn't agree more. It's easier to talk about living by faith than to do it. Instead of cringing in fear over what might, could, or should happen, a person who lives by faith steps out and trusts God. Boards can learn to do that too. When the board has determined that a course of action is right, it doesn't have to wait until every piece of the puzzle falls into place. It needs to act on what it knows. God will begin to fill in the blanks.

Fear

The worst danger we face is the danger of being paralyzed by doubts and fears. This danger is brought on by those who abandon faith and sneer at hope. It is brought on by those who spread cynicism and distrust and try to blind us to the great chance to do good for all mankind.

—Harry S. Truman

Optimize

Pastor Mark says we should "look for ways to build up, strengthen, and move forward." We need to "focus on the possibilities, rather than the problems."

Unquestionably, focusing on the problems will lead to discouragement, disappointment, and dismay. Concentrating on the possibilities is like putting a magnifying glass to a dry leaf. The sun shining through the magnifying glass causes the leaf to smoke, smolder, and finally burst into flames. Concentrating on what is possible instead of what is problematic tends to set your ideas on fire. It focuses your attention on how big God is instead of how big the problems are.

Argue

To argue means to provide the reasons why you're for or against something, and this can and should be done constructively. A healthy board is able to express a variety of viewpoints without coming unglued. Board members welcome different ideas, knowing that eventually they will settle on the best. Different viewpoints may well mean disagreements, yet mature people learn how to agreeably disagree. They know how important it is to "keep the unity of the Spirit through the bond of peace" (Eph. 4:3).

People with closed minds cannot handle this kind of discussion. Divergent viewpoints spell trouble in their minds. They find it hard to tolerate opinions that differ from their own. But such an attitude operates from a position of arrogance, as if only I have the right idea. Often we can piggyback on the ideas of others and come up with a solution that is better than any individual opinion that has been expressed.

Respond

The test of a board's character is in how it deals with difficult situations. Most of us don't like the word *discipline*, especially when it applies to the behavior of church members. But boards sometimes have to wrestle with such problems, in which a church member must be disciplined. Or it may not be a matter of discipline as much as a church member has been victimized and turns to the church for help.

Whatever the issues are, Pastor Mark believes we can discover the quality of the board by observing how it responds to difficult issues with wisdom, compassion, courage, and faith. He is right.

Decide

Sooner or later, the board has to make a decision. It can only analyze a situation for so long until it experiences paralysis by analysis. Don't allow uncertainty to paralyze the board. Gather all the facts and make the best decision possible. The alternative is an unproductive board that is a detriment to the church.

Business philosopher Jim Rohn compares making decisions to an "internal civil war. Conflicting armies of emotions, each with its own arsenal of reasons, battle each other for supremacy of our minds. And our resulting decisions, whether bold or timid, well thought out or impulsive, can either set the course of action or blind it."[8]

Decisions

Encouraging board members to make informed, intelligent decisions is actually one way to develop character. H. Van Anderson said, "The moment a question comes to your mind, see yourself mentally taking hold of it and disposing of it. In that moment is your choice made. Thus you learn to take the path to the right. Thus you learn to become the decider and not the vacillator. Thus you build character."

A More Productive Role

Fortunately, Gene proved to be capable of lifting his sights beyond simply being a watchdog and found a more productive role on the church board. While still conservative and suspicious of too much change too fast, he was open-minded enough to recognize a good idea, even though it was a new idea.

He not only fulfilled his role as a governor, but he also became as good an ambassador as the church had. His concern that the church might drift away from its moorings actually grew out of a sincere love for the church. He expressed that love not only in his official positions, but also by inviting others and spreading good words about the church.

In addition, he became a consultant for the pastor, who trusted his wisdom and maturity. His financial support of the church grew as he was able to increase it, and he and his wife even decided to remember the church in the final disposition of their estate when that time came.

Action Steps

1. What roles are your current board members filling? Rate their effectiveness in these roles.
2. Think about the four roles suggested by David Hubbard. How do your various board members currently fit into these four roles?
3. How are your board members functioning relative to the five action words in the acrostic B-O-A-R-D?

3

EXPECTATIONS
ESTABLISHING EXPECTATIONS FOR CHURCH BOARDS

*The pastor and board members need to have their
expectations on the same page.*

Steve, a brand new board member, was excited as he drove into
the church parking lot. "This is going to be great," he thought as
he turned off the ignition and pocketed the keys. "I've only been part
of Trinity Church for a year, but to be elected a board member . . ."
His thoughts trailed off as Sam, the church treasurer, entered the
building at the same time.

"Hey, Sam, how's it going?"

"Great, Steve, and welcome! I hope you enjoy your experience
as a board member."

"Thanks, I'm looking forward to it."

They entered the board room and each poured some coffee into
a Styrofoam cup before settling into his chair.

Pastor John called the meeting to order, read some Scripture,
and gave a few devotional thoughts, before saying, "As our first
item of business, I have a letter to read."

He unfolded a piece of paper and proceeded to read his resignation. Steve sat in shock. He felt like someone could have knocked him over with the proverbial feather. He had grown in his appreciation of the pastor, his sermons, and his warmth as a shepherd. But now, as the resignation letter continued, he came to grips with the fact that a larger church had contacted Pastor John to offer him a position as senior minister. And he had decided to accept.

So began months of meetings when the major order of business was the search for a new pastor. Steve realized his expectations when he became a board member were completely unrealistic. His bright-eyed enthusiasm at the honor of being part of the church leadership had dulled into an acceptance of the heavy responsibility that goes with such service.

Unrealistic Expectations

For those who have never been part of a church board, expectations may be realistic or not, depending on the length of their involvement with the church, knowledge of church matters, experience in serving on other nonprofit boards, or understanding of how a church board functions. For those with prior experience, their expectations may not be accurate about how this particular church board functions.

Unrealistic expectations in the mind of the new board member are exposed by five realities of the church board.

Needs and Challenges Facing the Board

A new board member may not know what the board grapples with, especially the challenges and needs that are unique to the church. If a novice board member has simply been coming to church, enjoying the worship services, and volunteering occasionally in some ministry of the church, he or she may not have been exposed to the nitty-gritty, behind-the-scenes realities of church life.

In truth, not every church is facing major challenges in its day-to-day life. In some churches, finances are adequate to cover the needs, staff positions are filled, volunteers are in sufficient supply, and the church is humming along rather nicely. But in other churches, new board members walk into their responsibility unaware that the church is operating on a shoestring, the pastor is ready to resign and the next several months are going to be spent in a pastoral search process, or a personality conflict is about to explode that will have church members taking sides.

If the new board member is resilient and happens to believe, along with Henry J. Kaiser, that "problems are only opportunities in work clothes,"[1] he or she will accept the challenges with faith and confidence. Or the new member may have to pray, along with

Challenges

The only task worth doing is one that is well-nigh impossible.

—Edward Land

Peter Marshall, former chaplain of the Senate, "When we long for life without difficulties, remind us that oaks grow strong in contrary winds and diamonds are made under pressure."[2]

Time Commitment

A newly elected person may not realize the time commitment expected of a board member. Some boards function smoothly, meetings hum along like a well-oiled machine, and people go home smiling and happy. Others lurch and jerk as if water has gotten into the fuel line. Meetings extend for three or four hours. Members wake up the next morning, bleary-eyed from lack of sleep.

A colleague assumed a new pastorate at a church that had functioned for more than a year without a senior pastor. In his denomination, the pastor serves as chair of the board. So in the absence of a pastor, a lay leader had valiantly chaired the meetings. But attendance dipped, finances declined, low morale set in, and the board probably over-managed the situation, meeting every week for long hours. When the new pastor arrived, the board was hungry for pastoral leadership and felt greatly relieved when he conducted shorter meetings once a month, and adjourned the board meetings at a reasonable time.

Time

Everything requires time. It is the one truly universal condition. All work takes place in time and uses up time. Yet most people take for granted this unique, irreplaceable, and necessary resource. Nothing else, perhaps, distinguishes effective executives as much as their tender loving care of time.

—Peter Drucker

Many board members—even long-term ones—have unrealistic expectations about time, whether board meetings are long or short.

Church Finances

When adequate money flows every week into the church's offering plates, sitting on the board may include hearing a treasurer's report in which the balances are positive, and no problems are apparent. However, if finances are tight and the treasurer struggles to make ends meet, board meetings may become tense. In fact, the majority of a board's time may consist of hearing the report, and responding to the unpleasant fact that income is not meeting expenses.

Some board meetings degenerate into micromanagement of the church's finances, with the board trying to oversee in minute detail the expenditure of every penny. Treasurers may become defensive. Pastors may become impatient. Board meetings may deteriorate into accusations of who is to blame for the tight financial situation.

When board members do not understand that dealing with finances is part of the responsibility of a board member and that keeping a positive attitude about the church and its ministry is one key way to address the problem, they may become discouraged. "This is not what I signed up for," more than one board member has muttered to him- or herself.

Strategic Planning

Many board members are not skilled in strategic planning and may not have given it a great deal of thought. If their work involves taking orders and doing as they're told with little room for input or creativity, it may not require much planning beyond showing up and putting in an eight-hour shift.

Without previous experience, they may not have realized, "If you always do what you've always done, you will always get what you've always got!" The way out of a rut, of doing the same thing the same way for years on end, is to develop a plan. A process of strategic planning helps a church move beyond where it is and move toward a preferred future.

Blessed is the board member whose pastor leads the way in planning strategically for the future. Some board members, without such leadership, realize there is a better way than stagnating, but through loyalty to the church they stick it out without complaint.

Others, feeling trapped in a stagnant situation, may simply fly off to another congregation.

If a pastor is not skilled in strategic planning but can tap the resources of creative laypersons, he or she can initiate change and promote positive plans. A layperson skilled in planning can be invaluable to a pastor who is wise enough to tap into this resource.

Personality Interaction

An inexperienced person may take a seat on a church board, expecting everyone to behave with civility toward other board members. And this is a legitimate expectation . . . in a perfect world! In the real world, however, board members have been known to fly off the handle or sit and sulk if they don't get their own way.

So, while it is legitimate to expect board members to act with a certain amount of decorum, this expectation needs to be balanced with the understanding that people are human. They sometimes do not behave their best. Instead, they surrender to their human inclinations. Especially when two strong-willed persons are members of the same board, conflicts may result. As someone observed, "If any two people hold exactly the same opinion all the time, one of them is unnecessary!" Another pointed out that when two live wires touch each other, sparks result!

The Protégé, the Ruler, and the Villain

Several biblical characters provide examples of persons who encountered unfulfilled expectations.

Balance of Power

When Barnabas and Paul left Antioch of Syria and set out on their first missionary journey, they took with them John Mark, a young cousin of Barnabas. Their first stop was the island of Cyprus, home territory for Barnabas (Acts 4:36). John Mark only stayed with Barnabas and Paul until they left Cyprus and arrived on the southern shores of Asia Minor, at a place called Perga in Pamphylia, what we would call Turkey today. When Luke described their journey to this new destination, he said, "From Paphos, Paul and his companions sailed to Perga" (Acts 13:13). Prior to this time, it had always been "Barnabas and Saul." From this point on, Luke referred to the missionary party mostly as "Paul and Barnabas," using Paul's Greek name and putting him in the position of prominence.

Did this change of leadership disturb John Mark? Did Mark, Barnabas's protégé, resent Paul's boldness and what seemed to be Paul's dominance over Barnabas? We do not know. Possibly, Mark simply became homesick. Maybe he was "unable to stand the rigors of pioneer missionary travel, or was fearful of the wild mountain country before them."[3]

Perhaps John Mark was surprised at Paul's determination to preach to the Gentiles, giving them equal opportunity with the Jews. Maybe Mark was reluctant to embrace the idea of bringing Gentiles into the faith. Paul may have spelled out his convictions in such forceful terms that Mark couldn't accept them and decided to turn back.

Whatever the reasons, Mark returned to Jerusalem, apparently not having fulfilled what was expected of him. Like some board members who accept election only to discover that the balance of power on the board is not what they expected, Mark turned back in disappointment. Sometimes new board members are not yet clear on the agenda, purpose, and mission of the church. When pastors clearly outline their plans, they do not meet the board members' expectations. Perhaps like Mark, the board members resign, saying, "This is not what I signed up for."

Single-Minded Dedication

Another Bible character whose expectations were unfulfilled was the one known as the rich young ruler. Mark said he was rich (Mark 10:22); Matthew told us he was young (Matt. 19:20); and Luke declared he was a ruler (Luke 18:18). The young man came to Jesus asking, "What must I do to inherit eternal life?"

Jesus responded by saying, "You know the commandments: 'Do not commit adultery, do not murder, do not steal, do not give false testimony, honor your father and mother.'" The young man boasted he had kept all these since he was a boy. Jesus told him, "You still lack one thing. Sell everything you have and give to the poor, and you will have treasure in heaven. Then come, follow me" (Luke 18:20–22).

At this, the young man became very sad because he was quite wealthy. Giving up his riches represented a greater price than he was prepared to pay. Like others who have approached God across the centuries, he did not have singleness of mind and heart. He wanted to gain eternal life, yet he wanted to cling to his riches. This is not an indictment of riches, but a caution against a divided heart.

We expect our board members to devote themselves to the work of the church. We understand that people have jobs, families, and hobbies. There is nothing wrong with any of that. But when a person accepts the responsibility of serving on the church board, a certain level of commitment is expected. I have known some wonderful people who tended to saddle up and ride off in all directions, dividing their time, attention, and loyalty. At least for the time a board member serves in that capacity, he or she must make such service a top priority.

Pride Precedes a Fall

One of the great villains of the Old Testament provides a third example of unfulfilled expectations. Haman, the archenemy of Mordecai in the book of Esther, strutted through the streets, full of pride until he met Mordecai. Ethnic animosity bristles in this story as Mordecai, a Jew, refused to bow before Haman, an Amalekite by ancestry.

Yet when Queen Esther invited King Xerxes and Haman to her banquet table, Haman could hardly contain himself. "I'm the only person Queen Esther invited to accompany the king to the banquet she gave," he boasted to his wife and friends. "And she has invited me along with the king tomorrow" (Est. 5:12). Little did he know that the banquet would provide the backdrop for a confrontation that would send him to the gallows.

I know of no board members so proud, deceitful, and as despicable as Haman, the veritable face of evil. But I have known board members who swelled with pride over their perceived importance. A colleague told me of one man who boasted that he would be elected to the board in the upcoming election. But a relative newcomer was elected instead, leaving the boastful board member embarrassed and chagrined.

Pride

Three tests to see whether we have succumbed to the sin of pride are:

1. The test of precedence. How do we react when someone else is selected for the office we expected to have?
2. The test of sincerity. We may often say self-critical things about ourselves, but how do we feel when others say them?
3. The test of criticism. Do we become hostile and resentful in our hearts when someone criticizes us? Do we criticize the critic?

If we are honest, when we measure ourselves by the life of our Lord who humbled himself even to death on a cross, we cannot but be overwhelmed with the tawdriness and shabbiness, and even the vileness, of our hearts.

—J. Oswald Sanders

Carnal pride has no place in the heart of a board member. No one should aspire to the position simply to satisfy his or her ego.

Fortunately, most board members do not have the negative motives of our biblical examples. But a warning is in order, lest any of us be led astray.

Expectations to Model

Whether written or unwritten, every church has a set of expectations for its board members. In some cases, the pastor will sit down with prospective board members and go over the written expectations to be sure they understand. In other churches, members may nominate from the floor persons they assume will follow expectations that are generally understood, but not necessarily written. Still other churches are just so happy to have someone fill the positions that they ask no questions. Some larger churches prepare written biographical information on each nominee for members to study prior to an election of board members.

Years ago, denominational executive Dr. Ronald D. Kelly wrote an article on the expectations of a local board member.[4] In it he specified a number of characteristics that many churches expect their board members to model.

A Model of Church Attendance

Churches expect their board members to attend the normal and regularly scheduled services and activities. If they find they cannot do so, there is an expectation in many churches that such persons will have the integrity to resign or not let their names run in the first place. Board members' attendance at the various regularly scheduled services and functions of the church lends credence to the importance of those activities.

A Model of Giving

In many churches, the expectation is that board members will set an example by tithing their income. In other words, they give 10 percent of their income in support of the church and its ministries. If the church is involved in a capital stewardship campaign, they are expected to give generously to the cause. Again, if they have not been able to get their finances in order to do this, the expectation is that they will resign to make room for those who can set a better example.

Churches do not publicize who gives what, so the board members are on their honor to fulfill this expectation. But people of integrity will do their best, even if it means giving sacrificially, in order to support the church they serve.

A Model in Christian Lifestyle

Every denomination or church group has its own expectations as to what constitutes right living. Whatever those qualities are, board members are expected to model them. These are the characteristics that the church has deemed the most positive witness to non-Christians. They exemplify the ideal Christian life. They provide the best example for new believers who are part of the group.

A Model of Ministry Involvement

Board members serve as models of involvement in practical ministry. They may teach a class, sing on the worship team, serve as ushers or youth sponsors, or lead visitation teams or recovery groups. In some way, they serve beyond simply sitting on the board.

This provides a model for others. They are willing to get their hands dirty in the actual work of ministry, not just sit in the ivory tower and hand out decisions.

Role Models

Those who model the right qualities are in reality role models.

Some of the most important people in my life would be shocked to learn that they were role models. They weren't celebrities, or even particularly accomplished. But they had some quality that I admired, that made me want to be like them.

—Donn Moomaw

A Model of Forward Thinking

Along with the pastor, board members understand the church's purpose and core values. They have a strong desire to help the church move to the next level, to fulfill God's purpose for the church in its community, and to see the church reach its community for Christ. They believe in the direction the church is moving, and they are excited about the possibilities.

Not everyone is ready to accept the responsibility to serve as a model in these ways. If members are not ready, no one should force them. After all, Paul said that regarding the appointment of church leaders, we should be careful about promoting people too soon. He said a leader should not be "a novice, lest being lifted up with pride he fall into the condemnation of the devil" (1 Tim. 3:6 KJV).

But just because persons are not ready to fulfill the expectations of a board member does not mean they will never serve. Put them on a list of people to be discipled. Watch them. Stay close to them. In time, they may be ready to become a model for God's people.

Perceptive Questions

Some churches ask prospective board members to provide answers that reveal their expectations and understanding of crucial matters concerning the church.

The Church's Purpose and Mission

For instance, one query may be: "In a few words, give your understanding of the purpose and mission of the church." Most pastors are happy to welcome new people, especially those who are already believers, who know how to teach or usher or serve in some other capacity.

But many people come to a new church with their own agendas. Though they appear to be open to the church's way of doing things, they have definite, established opinions about what the church should be doing and how it should operate. These may or may not be in line with the new church's purpose and mission.

Asking some strategic questions can help a pastor avoid the error of putting new people into positions of responsibility too soon. Better to move slowly and find out whether there is agenda harmony than to move too fast and subsequently have to make painful changes in personnel.

The Church's Strengths and Weaknesses

Another question may be this: "What do you consider the church's greatest strengths?" A colleague told me about meeting the visiting adult son of one of his members. The son happened to be a member of a church in California whose pastor was well-known for his biblical sermons and national influence.

"It must be great to attend worship every Sunday and hear Pastor Jones [not his real name] speak," the pastor said.

"Well, we enjoy his messages," responded the visitor, "but we would attend that church whether he was the pastor or not."

"Really? Tell me why."

"We love the small group we have joined. That's the real reason we attend that church."

The young man was unknowingly commenting on a strength of that church. To the onlooker, one strength was the excellent preaching and teaching of the senior pastor. But to an insider, another strength was the small group ministry or emphasis on discipleship.

To learn such information from prospective board members tells you a great deal about where they think the church is now and what their expectations might be for helping chart the church's future.

You may gain similar information by asking a follow-up question: "What do you consider the church's weaknesses?" This may reveal information and opinions that are uncomfortable to hear. But how significant to have a prospective board member tell you where they think the gaps are in ministry that need to be filled with new programs, personnel, or emphases.

Someone observed that the greatest cause of disagreement on church boards is the difference in priorities among board members.

Asking strategic questions before welcoming people into leadership will help discover what their priorities are.

The Greatest Challenges

Another important question is this: "What do you think are the greatest challenges facing the church over the next six months?" This question will tell you whether your prospective board members have been paying attention. Do they know what is going on in the congregation? Do they understand the direction the church is taking, the major snags that have been encountered, and the difficult hills the church will have to climb in the next few months?

Expectations of the Pastor

Here's another enlightening question about board members' expectations: "What are the three areas/roles you feel are most important for the senior pastor to perform?" We have all seen studies in which pastors rank ten or twelve items of pastoral work as their priority. When laypersons rank those same items, the results are seldom the same. Preaching is almost always ranked high on the pastor's list; but a layperson may think, for instance, that care and counseling are much more important.

Pastoral Expectations

While pastor of a Florida church, Thom Raines asked his deacons to write down the number of hours they thought he should spend on his various pastoral duties. When he tabulated the results, here's what their expectations were:

Sermon preparation	18 hours
Administration	18 hours
Hospital/home visitation	15 hours
Prayer	14 hours
Worship/preaching	10 hours
Outreach visitation	10 hours
Counseling	10 hours
Community activities	5 hours
Denominational tasks	5 hours
Church meetings	5 hours
Miscellaneous	4 hours

That's a total of 114 hours (out of 168 hours in a week)!

While there may always be differences in the way pastors and laypeople see the pastor's responsibilities, a dialogue can be the beginning of better understanding. I don't fully understand the way my medical doctor spends his time or why, because I am a layperson when it comes to medicine. But I do trust him to do what is best for me when I show up at his office.

Personal Ministry beyond the Board

Another helpful question to ask a prospective board member is: "What kinds of ministry in the church do you have beyond your service to the board?" If we expect board members to serve in ways that stretch them beyond sitting on the board, it will be good to explore this topic before they assume a board position. A closely related question is: "What are your spiritual gifts?" Obviously, you want all your members to serve in the area of their giftedness if possible.

This is not an exhaustive list of the questions you can ask a prospective board member, but they are among the most important ones. Clarifying board members' expectations of the church and the church's expectations of its board members are key elements in avoiding misunderstanding and conflict in the months and years to come.

A Maturing Experience

In spite of the shock he felt when the pastor resigned at his first board meeting, Steve enjoyed his term of service on the board. While board service soon lost the luster it had when he walked across the parking lot and entered the building for his first meeting, he matured in his service. He came to understand that board service was both a responsibility and a privilege.

His expectations changed as his understanding grew. He came to know and appreciate the other members of the board. As a group, they rose to the occasion and matured as they took on the responsibility of finding a new pastor. Steve not only appreciated his fellow members; they appreciated him. He was reelected and continued to render good service to the church.

Initial expectations gave way to informed expectations, and what he expected of himself became more realistic as well.

Action Steps

1. How does your church currently assess the expectations of prospective board members? What can you do to provide a better experience in this area?

2. What unrealistic expectations do you feel your current board members hold? What could be done to bring expectations more into line with reality?

3. Assess how well your current board members are modeling the church's expectations of its board. What can you do to improve the board's performance in this area?

4

Business
Running Effective
Board Meetings

*Planning is the pastor's best friend for running
effective board meetings.*

Richard Wallarab envisioned a meeting of the board that
consists of the apostles who followed Jesus:

PETE: This meeting has been called at the request of Matt, John,
  Tom, and Little Jim. Bart, will you please open with prayer?

BART: Almighty God, we ask your blessing on all we do and
  say and earnestly pray that you will see our side as your side.
  Amen.

PETE: Jesus, we have been following you around for some time,
  and we are getting concerned about the attendance figures.
  Tom, how many were on the hill yesterday?

TOM: Thirty-seven.

PETE: It's getting to be ridiculous. You're going to have to pep
  things up. We expect things to happen.

JOHN: I'd like to suggest you pull off some more miracles. That
  walking on the water bit was the most exciting thing I have

ever seen, but only a few of us saw it. If a thousand or so had a chance to witness it, we would have more than we could handle on the hill.

LITTLE JIM: I agree. The healing miracles are terrific, but only a limited number really get to see what has happened. Let's have more water to wine, more fish and chips (it never hurts to fill their stomachs), still more storms, give more signs. This is what the people need.

PETE: Right! And another thing, publicity is essential, and you tell half the people you cure to keep it quiet. Let the word get around.

MATT: I'm for miracles, but I want to hear a few stories I can understand. This "those who have ears to hear, let them hear" business just clouds the issue. You have to make it clear or most of us aren't going to be able to take anything home.

BIG JIM: I'd like to offer an order of service. First a story, then a big miracle, followed by an offering, then maybe a saying or something, followed by a small miracle to bring them back next time. Oh yes, and a prayer if you like.

TOM: We have to do something.

LITTLE JIM: That's for sure. Attendance has been awful.

JUDAS: I'd like to say if we're going to continue to meet in this upper room, we ought to do something about the carpet.[1]

Board Meetings That Drag

The above scenario Wallarab painted is apocryphal. It didn't really happen, but we can all identify with it because it sounds scarily similar to so many meetings we have attended.

John Kenneth Galbraith spoke for a great many people when he said, "Meetings are indispensable when you don't want to do anything."[2]

Committee meetings (and board meetings are similar, except they sound more important) are notorious for wasting people's time. But why?

Lack of Agenda

Many meetings have sputtered and stalled because nobody planned an agenda. It isn't just true of churches; it's true in the corporate world as well. There's the weekly staff meeting. It's always on the schedule. It comes around once a week, ready or not.

And after all, everybody is busy. We have a general idea what's supposed to happen, but Tuesday creeps up again and there just isn't time to put together a formal agenda. So we decide to wing it. Again.

After a while, people know when you're running on empty. They realize you're circling the field but you can't find a good place to land the plane, a good place to land your thought, or how to move on to something that is actually important.

Having an agenda goes a long way toward solving this problem. We'll talk more about that later in this chapter.

Unclear Purpose

Having a meeting just for the sake of having a meeting is a good way to derail it before you get started. Just because it's on the calendar is not a good reason to have a meeting. It's like somebody asked a friend of mine once: "Do you preach because you have something to say or because you have to say something?" Pastors have to say something every Sunday. God help us if we don't have anything worthwhile to say!

The same goes for meetings. Do you have meetings because you have plans to pursue, goals to achieve, and things to work out together? Or do you meet just because the calendar says it's time?

Big Goals

Big goals get big results. No goals get no results or somebody else's results.

— Mark Victor Hansen

If you have a purpose for meeting— beyond reviewing minutes from the last meeting—you can inspire people rather than wear them out. It's the difference between leaving the meeting motivated or drained.

Afflicted by Boredom

A board meeting that is going nowhere and has no sense of purpose will ultimately be afflicted by boredom. Meetings often include the boredom of boards and the commitment of committees. But they need not bog down in boredom. Good planning, as we shall see later, will eliminate the affliction of boredom and will fuse new life into your meetings.

The Spiritual Side of Planning

Successful board meetings are all about organizing people and projects. In every church are people who need to minister and be ministered to. There are projects that need to be organized, staffed, and accomplished. Behind all of this ministry and project accomplishment is a pastor and board who are thinking things through and organizing for action.

In my book *Practical Guide for Pastoral Ministry*, I gave several keys to a successful board meeting.[3] These keys were based on biblical truths.

╌╾═ ═╾╌

Will to Succeed

The will to succeed is important, but what's more important is the will to prepare.

—Bobby Knight

For instance, the Bible is all about planning. You can't go far in the Scriptures without seeing the organizing hand of God and his people. One of the bright lights of the Old Testament is Jeremiah 29:11, which reads, "'For I know the plans I have for you,' declares the LORD, 'plans to prosper you and not to harm you, plans to give you hope and a future.'"

Planning in Creation

No one should be surprised to know that God plans ahead. When we read, "In the beginning God created the heavens and the earth" (Gen. 1:1), and we see that he created certain things on the first day, other things on the second, still more on the third, and so on, we see a God of organization and planning.

Why couldn't he have made it all happen at once? I suppose he could have, but his creative mind recognized that before plants existed, they would need light and water to survive and thrive. So he saw to it that light and water existed before he began the vegetation-producing process.

Planning in Worship

When God directed Moses regarding the preparation of a place of worship, he left nothing to chance. In Exodus 26, God gave Moses detailed instructions regarding the types of materials he should use. God gave precise numbers for the size of the curtains, the quantity of gold clasps, the number of tent frames, and the distance one thing should be from another—even down to the color of yarn he should use, the number of gold hooks, and the bronze bases. God made sure the instructions were explicit.

You will find similar details in 1 Chronicles 28, which gives us the plans David acquired for the building of the temple. Although God did not permit David to build it, he did allow David to assemble the materials for his son Solomon. So David carried out his part in the entire planning process.

Planning in Salvation

When God planned for a way to save his people from their sins, he developed the plans even before the foundation of the world. As Paul wrote: "For he chose us in him before the creation of the world to be holy and blameless in his sight. In love he predestined us to be adopted as his sons through Jesus Christ, in accordance with his pleasure and will—to the praise of his glorious grace, which he has freely given us in the One he loves. . . . In him we were also chosen, having been predestined according to the plan of him who works out everything in conformity with the purpose of his will" (Eph. 1:4–6, 11).

Jesus advised planning as a part of our normal method of operation. "Suppose one of you wants to build a tower," he said. "Will he not first sit down and estimate the cost to see if he has enough money to complete it?" (Luke 14:28).

Planning to Spread the Gospel

The apostle Paul was an example of planning. He traveled from place to place, not haphazardly, but according to a plan. He not only visited the cities of Iconium, Derbe, and Lystra, establishing a church in each, but he retraced his steps and went back to each one. His purpose? He was "strengthening the disciples and encouraging them to remain true to the faith" (Acts 14:22).

Paul wrote to the Romans about his plans. He had never been to that city, the center of political power and the military headquarters of the civilized world. But it was not for lack of trying. He admitted to the Romans, "I have often been hindered from coming to you" (Rom. 15:22).

Delays did not dampen his plans. He said, "I have been longing for many years to see you, [and] I plan to do so when I go to Spain. I hope to visit you while passing through and to have you assist me on my journey there, after I have enjoyed your company for a while" (Rom. 15:23–24).

So Paul revealed how extensively he planned. He not only made it his goal to visit Rome, but he also planned to go to Spain. But he would not go to Spain before he enjoyed the Romans' company. This implies that he planned to stay with them and probably includes the expectation that he would be the recipient of their hospitality (food, lodging, fellowship). In addition, upon leaving Rome, he would take with him the wherewithal (financial means) provided by the Roman Christians (which is what he meant by "have you assist me on my journey there").

So if anyone thinks planning for a board meeting is not spiritual, take another look at the Bible. It is full of planning and examples of organization.

Planning on Purpose

Since meetings consume so much of our time and energy, they ought to be meaningful. But this does not happen by accident. If you want your meetings to be more than time-fillers—or perhaps more accurately time-wasters—you need to plan.

Preparation

Some anonymous comic, fond of alliteration, pointed out that "proper prior planning prevents pitifully poor performance." In other words, more church board meetings would be more productive if more planning went into their preparation.

A colleague confessed to me that he finally figured out the reason why he dreaded his church board meetings so much: He didn't spend enough time planning them. This fits what business philosopher Jim Rohn said, "The reason why most people face the future with apprehension instead of anticipation is because they don't have it well-designed."[4]

In the Canadian northland, where very few people live, they say there are two seasons: winter and July. Before some of the roads were paved, they were soft in the rainy season. When the frost came, the ground hardened into whatever shape the cars and trucks had left it. In other words, it was full of ruts. At the beginning of one such road, an interesting sign said it all: "Be careful what rut you choose. You'll be in it for the next twenty miles."

Plodding along in ruts may describe what some church board meetings are like, but all that could be avoided with good, sound planning. By taking the time to think things through, we prepare ourselves as well as our plans.

Benjamin Disraeli, prime minister of Great Britain in the 1870s, said, "One secret of success in life is for a man to be ready for his opportunity when it comes."[5] What a shame if a man or woman misses a great opportunity in life all because he or she failed to plan. So away with excuses! Get busy and plan that next board meeting.

Organization

Good planning leads to good organization. In the next section, we

Preparation

Don Beveridge and Jeffery P. Davidson said that "preparation dramatically increases your chances of achieving, excelling, and getting ahead in business. If you shortcut preparation, you've got a very good chance of striking out. Preparation is the most important element of success. Without it, you won't even play the game."

While this may be true in business, it is also true in preparing to lead effective board meetings.

will address one specific way to organize your agenda. But for now consider the following elements that will help any board meeting run more smoothly.

The Agenda. A well-thought-out agenda is like a road map for your meeting. Your agenda is important for at least two practical reasons. First, it will keep your meeting on track. If you go into a meeting without a plan, others will plan it for you. They will ask a question, bring up a topic of interest, or express an objection that may or may not further the cause. It's never a good practice to open up the meeting for suggestions as to what you should cover. You will get a lot of ideas, but they will be based on competing agendas from various board members, and you will lose the opportunity to have a meeting that actually accomplishes something that furthers the cause.

The second practical reason for having an agenda is that it prevents all-nighters. If you don't know where you're going, you won't know when you arrive. Thus it's hard to know when to quit. You keep hoping you will accomplish something worthwhile so you can close the meeting with a sense of satisfaction. But without an agenda it is not very likely to happen.

Room Preparation. Has the thermostat been set to a comfortable level? Have refreshments been prepared? Is the lighting adequate? What about paper and pens? Have you positioned a copy of the agenda at every place? If you plan to use multimedia, have you tested it? All of these elements, if prepared adequately, can make your participants comfortable and improve the quality of the meeting. If you don't give these matters any thought, your participants may be uncomfortable and in a bad mood throughout the meeting.

Minutes. Most boards have a duly-elected recording secretary. If not, one should be appointed at the outset of every meeting. He or she should not try to record all the discussion. The secretary should record the main actions taken during the meeting, then type, print, and distribute the minutes at the following meeting. Memories are short and may be faulty. A good set of minutes will help remind everyone of the important things discussed and decided at the previous meeting.

Devotions. Because yours is a Christian meeting, it is appropriate to read a passage from God's Word and pray, seeking God's will for the meeting. You may involve others in the discussion during the devotional time. This gives them an opportunity to communicate.

Wrap-Up. By summarizing the board's actions near the end of the meeting, you give the board members a sense of accomplishment, and it gives you as the chair the opportunity to end the meeting on a positive note. Be sure to note the time and place for the next meeting.

Communication

Communication is a two-way street. For the board meeting to be successful, the members must have a chance to express themselves. As chair you may be tempted to dominate the meeting. By setting the agenda and presenting the matters to be discussed, you may fall into the trap of doing all the talking. Resist this and encourage others to express themselves. You may not agree with everything that is said and the board members may not agree with each other, but eventually, you will achieve consensus.

Compassion

Your meeting is about and for the church, and its purpose is to benefit the church. Taking care of your members and reaching out to the community in effective ministry should be the motivation behind every program, ministry, and building enterprise. Ask the Holy Spirit to warm the hearts of your board members and keep them sensitive to the needs of your congregation.

Communication

You cannot speak that which you do not know. You cannot share that which you do not feel. You cannot translate that which you do not have. And you cannot give that which you do not possess. To give it and to share it, and for it to be effective, you first need to have it. Good communication starts with good preparation.

—Jim Rohn

Organizing the Meeting

Your agenda may be complex, or it may be simple. You may have a heavy meeting with much to discuss or a light meeting with no weighty matters before you. Whatever the content of your meeting, it is helpful to organize it in such a way that you achieve the purpose of the meeting while keeping a great spirit of fellowship and camaraderie.

The following plan has helped many pastors prevent their board meetings from becoming monthly battles over turf or boring sessions that run on endlessly. Consider organizing your agenda around three items: information, study, and action.

Information Items

Information items are meant to be just that: information. They are not intended for discussion, debate, or decision. They simply inform. The minutes of last month's meeting are given for information. Upcoming events on the calendar are information items. Anything that simply informs without calling for a decision fits into this category. Information items are important; they just don't need to drag on for a half hour.

One thing that can help a great deal is if you place a copy of all reports and the agenda into the board members' hands on the Sunday prior to the meeting. This way they have a chance to read over most of the information items before they come to the meeting. They come already having thought about some of the things that will likely arise at the meeting.

Study Items

Study items go a step beyond information. They inform with the idea that members may eventually make a decision, but likely not at this time. Only in an emergency would a study item move to an action item all in one meeting.

One of my friends relates how he used to go to board meetings thoroughly prepared. He would present an issue and lay out all the pros and cons. Obviously, there would be more pros, because it was generally something he wanted to secure the board's approval to do. So he would inundate them with information, show all the advantages, and then call for a motion to take the action he proposed.

The problem was that the board members had not had time to process the information. What my eager friend had not stopped to realize is that he had spent days, perhaps weeks, thinking about his idea. It had time to marinate in his fertile mind. He had thought of all the objections, and he countered them with all the advantages, or so he thought. He could not imagine that anyone would object after his stellar presentation.

He had not considered that human nature does not like to be pushed. People don't like to be forced into a corner. They don't like to feel that they don't have options. Even if they are in favor of something, they get uneasy if they feel rushed into a decision. They're like the person to whom the telemarketer says, "This deal is only good for today. It expires in fifteen minutes."

My friend could have saved himself some heartburn if he had presented his great ideas as study items. He could have made it clear they were only going to consider it, discuss it, brainstorm about it, and toss around the possibilities. Sometimes it is necessary to bring

Prepare

Charles Lowery tells about Harry Houdini, considered by many to be America's great magician. He placed great emphasis on preparation and timing. He allowed a boxer to hit him full force in the stomach one day, but his timing was off a split second. He reeled and coughed, then told the boxer, "Not that way. I've got to get set. Now hit me." The boxer struck again and the magician's abdomen seemed like granite. However, ten days later, he died from the damage inflicted by the boxer's first blow. Lowery observes, "Sometimes life's going to hit you in the stomach. Prepare."

up something as a study item for several meetings in a row until you sense that you have consensus and people are ready to approve the idea.

You may use this idea with committee reports. Let the committee present all the facts. Get it all out in the open. Invite questions. Let your committee persons be the experts and provide the answers. If they don't have the answers, send them back to do some more research. If everyone understands that it's a study item and no action is going to be taken, everybody wins. The committee doesn't feel its research is in vain. The committee persons aren't offended because the board didn't like their ideas. And the board's input may even help to refine and improve them. Only after a matter has been fully discussed will it move to the action item stage.

Action Items

Action items are the issues on which you are ready to take action. Now it's time to make a decision. All sides have been looked at and every angle has been explored. Now you're ready to call for a motion and take a vote.

It's a good idea to use the rule of thumb that nothing can become an action item until it has been a study item for at least one previous meeting. As I said earlier, in case of an emergency, you can always suspend this rule. But once your board members get used to the idea of study items first, and then action items, they will be reluctant to force an issue until it has had plenty of exposure.

Here's one of the great advantages of this plan: It relieves the pressure. It removes the pressure from you as the chair, and it takes the pressure off the board members to make a decision before they're ready. You may actually go home after a board meeting with a smile on your face. You may actually begin to look forward to board meetings.

Being Effective

We have all been in one or more meetings that sounded eerily like that dysfunctional flight of fancy that was at the beginning of this chapter.

By planning ahead, preparing an agenda, giving serious thought to the meeting, and treating the board members with respect, they are released to do creative thinking and problem solving instead of wrangling about the color of the carpet. If a church is running smoothly, the board should not have to make many minor decisions. Many of those things should be cared for in the day-to-day operation of the church. Effective administration makes decisions at the lowest possible level. This frees up the board's time for the more serious matters.

Board meetings are meant to accomplish something. We should never be satisfied without accomplishing something worthwhile in each meeting. Albert Schweitzer said, "A man can only do what a man can do. But if he does that each day he can sleep at night and do it again the next day."[6] I might add, if those people pray, God can multiply their effectiveness. I hope it will be so in your experience making your board effective.

Action Steps

1. What are some of the unintended effects you have experienced in board meetings? What could you have done differently to make them more effective?

2. How long does it take you to plan most board meetings? What do you need to do differently to make your meetings more effective?

3. Review the agenda from your latest board meeting. Did you stick to it? Was it effective? How might it have been different if you had used the information, study, and action item list?

5

MOVEMENT
LEVERAGING BOARDS TO
STIMULATE PROGRESS

Progress occurs as we plan for it day by day.

Anthony Smith and three friends decided to fulfill a childhood dream and sail across the Atlantic—on a raft.

Sailing down the Mississippi with Huck Finn on a raft would be one thing, but sailing across the Atlantic? That requires a whole different set of skills.

It took more than two months to build the raft, which measured forty-three feet by twenty feet. On the platform, Mr. Smith built a cabin. The finished product was a curved, insulated, stainless steel hut with four solar panels and a wind turbine. Inside, the cabin contained four beds, an oven, and a communications desk—with GPS, a computer for e-mails, and an emergency distress system.

Under the platform were fourteen tubes to give the raft buoyancy. Five of them contained drinking water—two thousand liters of it. Their fresh food ran out after three weeks, but they used the oven to bake bread, and the men took turns cooking. Shepherd's pie, pasta dishes, and corned beef hash became the most popular items during their ten weeks at sea.

The all-British crew sailed from the Canary Islands, off the coast of Morocco and southwest of Spain, to St. Maarten's, an island in the Caribbean. Their original destination was the Bahamas, but strong winds blew them several hundred miles off course. Altogether, they spent sixty-six days at sea.

When the crew arrived in St. Maarten's, they were all sporting beards and were several pounds lighter than when they left home.

When asked why they would undertake the 2,600 mile adventure on "a tin can on a wooden plate," as they described it, Mr. Smith said, "The raft is more stable and buoyant than most yachts and less likely to capsize." A forty-foot sail powered the craft.

Did I mention that Mr. Smith is eighty-five-years-old and cannot walk without assistance since a van hit him in 2008? Naturally, many people told him he was crazy to attempt this trip at his age. He answered, "Age is irrelevant."[1]

Sailing across the Atlantic on a raft at the age of eighty-five is an achievement to say the least. We admire people like Mr. Smith, especially when we have trouble moving our church board off the same position it has held for the past twenty years.

That statement is only slightly cynical. Many church boards are wonderfully progressive, but enough are stuck in the past to give pastors headaches and ulcers well into the foreseeable future.

That Slippery Bottom Line

Activity is not the same as advancement. Posturing is not the same as progress. Movement is not the same as improvement. You can run in place on a treadmill and burn a lot of calories, but not make any progress. You can generate tons of activities meant to keep people busy, but when they are finished and exhausted, has your church advanced one inch toward its goals?

A pastor can only blame his or her church board for a lack of progress for so long. Then he or she must accept the responsibility of trying to bring the board into a position where its members desire progress and are tired of the status quo.

What Is the "Bottom Line"?

One of the problems we face, not only in churches, but in all nonprofit organizations, is the quandary of the bottom line. A friend told me about a church board member who served on the boards of several nonprofits. As a businessman, he was used to looking at the bottom line. Is there any profit? He became famous (or, more accurately, infamous) on those various boards for asking, "What's the bottom line?"

That is the problem in nonprofits: "Where is the bottom line?" In a business, profit and loss may not be the only means of judging performance, but they are concrete realities to which one can point.

How does one measure performance in a hospital emergency room, for instance? Is it based on how many patients one sees? Is it based on how fast the staff can respond to a patient once he or she enters the door? Is it based on how quickly people can be treated and either released or admitted? Is it based on how many heart attack victims survive?

As you can see, there are many questions to consider besides how much revenue the hospital is generating, especially if it is a nonprofit enterprise.

What Constitutes Progress?

The same thing is true in a church. Before you can talk about whether a board is making progress or not, you must decide, what constitutes progress. Do we say we are performing well if attendance is increasing? Or is it all about whether contributions increase? What if attendance increases and contributions do not? What if attendance increases among certain demographics but the church is losing regular contributors? How do you measure progress?

As the church looks at its various constituencies, it will face different ideas about what constitutes progress? Does the church have a great youth ministry? If so, what does that mean? Does it mean that attendance is growing among middle schoolers, high schoolers, and young adults? Does it mean that a certain percentage of young people are making commitments to Christ? Does it have anything to do with how many of them become involved in service projects, mission trips, or feel a call into full-time Christian service?

What about the church where the youth group has grown so much that the facilities are bursting at the seams but the group is just one big party? No life change is occurring. Is that success? Who decides?

Someone may object, "Church work is so hard to quantify. It's all about serving. If we faithfully preach the gospel, we have to leave the results in the Lord's hands. We can't control the results."

That observation has a certain amount of truth in it. Yet some nonprofits have learned how to measure progress. The Salvation Army, while doing a great deal of humanitarian work, is fundamentally a religious organization. "Nevertheless, it knows the percentage of alcoholics it restores to mental and physical health and the percentage of criminals it rehabilitates. It is highly quantitative."[2]

One of the responsibilities of the pastor is to lead his or her board into a true understanding of what constitutes progress. This will involve discussing what the bottom line means in that particular congregation. Such discussion may involve disagreement because people coming from different constituencies (youth, young adult, middle-aged, seniors) may see things differently and expect different results. Such disagreement is not a bad thing. In fact, if a board achieves consensus too quickly, it is usually a sign that members have not thought through all the issues involved.

Results

Work joyfully and peacefully, knowing that right thoughts and right efforts will inevitably bring about right results.

—James Allen

Paul's Insights into Progress

Those who are reluctant to measure results in a local church should reexamine the parable of the talents. Jesus told the story of a man who went on a journey and entrusted his property to his servants. He gave one five talents (worth more than a thousand dollars), another two talents, and a third servant only one talent, "each according to his ability" (Matt. 25:15). When the master returned, he was pleased that the servant with five talents had gained five more and the servant with two talents had gained two more.

However, when the servant with one talent admitted that he had hidden the talent in the ground to keep it safe, the master called the servant wicked and lazy. He chastised him for not at least putting the money on deposit with the bankers so it would earn interest.

Finally, he told the other servants to "throw that worthless servant outside, into the darkness, where there will be weeping and gnashing of teeth" (Matt. 25:30).

Obviously, results do matter. An Eastern proverb says, "Do not be afraid of going slowly; be afraid of standing still."

Making Progress as an Individual

I do not know whether the apostle Paul knew that proverb, but he exemplified it. He was not a person to stand still. He wanted to see progress. When you think of the sum total of his accomplishments in life, it was one of considerable movement. It is easy to trace three major missionary journeys in his lifetime. He invested his talents wisely for the Lord.

Even when he stayed in one place for a long time, Paul was making progress. When he was not traveling, he was preaching, teaching, and writing letters. In two of his letters—one to an individual and one to a church—he actually used the word *progress*.

To Timothy, he wrote, "Be diligent in these matters; give yourself wholly to them, so that everyone may see your progress" (1 Tim. 4:15). Be diligent in which matters? To what should Timothy give himself wholly? What was so important?

The entire fourth chapter of 1 Timothy provides context for these instructive words of Paul. Paul told Timothy to be diligent to:

- Beware of those who may abandon the faith and follow deceiving spirits (v. 1).
- Beware of hypocritical liars, whose consciences have been seared (v. 2).
- Beware of false teachers (v. 3).

- Recognize that everything God has created is good and is to be received with thanksgiving (v. 4).
- Teach positive truths to his people (v. 6).
- Watch out for godless myths (v. 7).
- Train himself to be godly (v. 7).
- Be an example for the believers (v. 12).
- Devote himself to the Scripture, preaching, and teaching (v. 13).
- Not neglect his gift (v. 14).
- Watch his life and doctrine closely (v. 16).
- Persevere (v. 16).

While most of Paul's warnings and injunctions were meant for Timothy personally, several of them were meant to guide him in his teaching, preaching, and influencing others. Timothy could disciple the leaders of the churches, adding value to their lives, and developing their faith. And we can do the same for our fellow church leaders today. As we strengthen them, we strengthen the church. As we encourage them, they become encouragers of others. As they grow spiritually, they become spiritual leaders of the congregation.

Making Progress as a Church

To the church at Philippi, Paul wrote, "Convinced of this, I know that I will remain, and I will continue with all of you for your progress and joy in the faith, so that through my being with you again your joy in Christ Jesus will overflow on account of me" (Phil. 1:25–26). What was Paul so convinced of that it was worth continuing in order that progress and joy might result?

The context reveals that great passage in which Paul said, "For to me, to live is Christ and to die is gain. If I am to go on living in the body, this will mean fruitful labor for me. Yet what shall I choose? I do not know! I am torn between the two: I desire to depart and be with Christ, which is better by far; but it is more necessary for you that I remain in the body" (Phil. 1:21–24).

Paul had such great confidence in the Lord that he believed if he were to die suddenly, he would be transported to glory. Yet he had such great love for the people to whom he ministered that he preferred to stay with them for the time being in order to see them make the progress that God had in mind for them.

A colleague told me that a denominational official called him and asked him to consider moving to a church in Canada. It would have meant uprooting his family and, as an American citizen, getting a green card in order to live and work in a foreign country. He was willing to do these things if he had felt it was God's will. After praying and weighing the options, he called the official and explained, "I am greatly honored that you would consider me for what is undoubtedly a wonderful opportunity and a great challenge. However, I feel that my relationship with this church is very crucial right now. The people finally all seem to be moving in the same direction. I would like to stay and see them make the progress I feel they are capable of making." To go would have been an honor. But it was more important for him to remain their shepherd. In the succeeding years, they did make considerable progress, and he felt his decision was vindicated.

These examples from Paul's writing remind us that whether we are talking about ourselves as individuals or as a corporate body, we need to see results. We need to make progress.

Every conscientious pastor wants to see his or her church make progress. Working with the board is one of the chief ways to see that happen. That's where decisions are made that affect the direction of the church. A pastor and a board working together in synchronized ministry can make the difference between progress, plateau, or decline.

Ambition

Keep away from people who try to belittle your ambitions. Small people always do that, but the really great make you feel that you, too, can become great.

—Mark Twain

Sowing and Reaping

Years ago I talked about sowing and reaping in an article I wrote entitled "The Law of the Harvest." The very idea of sowing and reaping is about results. If you invest your life appropriately, you will reap positive results. If you help your church board invest in the right things, they too will reap positive results. God promises to supply in response to our service. Jesus said, "Seek first his kingdom and his righteousness, and all these things will be given to you as well" (Matt. 6:33).

We Reap What We Invest

In nature the harvest comes only after sowing. In football the touchdown comes after the run or the pass. In science discovery comes after the experiment. The effort produces the effect. It's the same in the spiritual realm. The wise man wrote, "The wicked man earns deceptive wages, but he who sows righteousness reaps a sure reward" (Prov. 11:18).

In God's kingdom, our investments result in expectations. It's a matter of faith. We invest, and then we believe God for the return.

Be assured that no financial statement on earth will ever reflect a greater return on investment than what we will receive from our heavenly Father. Our returns will not always come in the form of dollars. There are more important things than monetary rewards: peace, love, joy, purpose, family, talents. The list of benefits is nearly endless, but it all begins with our personal investments.

One of the great things you can do for your board is to lead it in understanding that we reap what we invest. If you want to have a great children's ministry, you have to invest in finding the right people to lead the children's ministry. You have to be willing to invest dollars in developing the children's ministry. The same is true for youth, young adults, outreach, humanitarian programs, and missions. If you want to have a great staff, you have to invest in staff and their development. Whatever you want, you have to invest up front in order to reap the results you desire.

Sowing and Reaping

God has the tough end of the deal. What if, instead of planting the seed, you had to make the tree? That would keep you up late at night, trying to figure that one out.

—Jim Rohn

We Reap in God's Time

The wise man said, "There is a time for everything, and a season for every activity under heaven" (Eccl. 3:1). In the human realm, we're often on a predictable financial time clock. We live by quarterly or yearly reports. We circle April 15 on our calendars. We receive paychecks every two weeks.

But God is not necessarily on the same schedule. He rewards us in "due time." Peter wrote, "Humble yourselves, therefore, under God's mighty hand, that he may lift you up in due time" (1 Pet. 5:6).

God is not limited by earth's time or space. He looks beyond the immediate to the long-term. Throughout history, his prophecies and promises have been given when the time was right—and always right on time. God knows exactly what you need and when you need it. You may not see an immediate return on your investment of time, talent, or treasure, but it will come along right on schedule—God's schedule. Your job is to keep working and trust the Lord of the harvest.

One of the difficult things about ministry is what sometimes appears to be a lack of connection between what we sow and what we reap. We may work hard at investing ourselves, and the results don't come as soon as we think they should or with the impact we think they should. At other times, we experience great results, and we wonder, "What did I do? I don't know how that happened."

Be assured that if you reap results of which you did not plant, someone before you planted and you have the joy of reaping the harvest. God's timing is often a mystery. But do the right things anyway. Sow good seed anyway. Believe that God will bring his results in his time.

We Reap More Than We Invest

Jesus illustrated this principle in one of his parables. He told of some seed that fell on good soil where it produced a crop up to a hundred times what had been sown (see Matt. 13:8). God doesn't reward us with just what we deserve or even just enough. He always provides more.

Heaven hasn't been downsized. God's resources aren't subject to budget cuts. So when you're on the expecting side of a heavenly investment, you can look for a lavish reward. Jesus said, "If you then, though you are evil, know how to give good gifts to your children, how much more will your Father in heaven give the Holy Spirit to those who ask him!" (Luke 11:13).

When you invest with the Savior, your resources are secure. The law of the harvest is still in effect, and there will be a reward.

Making Progress on Purpose

Once in a while, good things just happen. It is not the obvious result of something we've done. However, there may be a connection between what we did and the positive results, but we can't see the connection. Most of the time, good things happen because we have a plan. But what should the plan be? Here are some ideas that can work in a church of any size.

Define Your Mission

Every church's mission should be some variation of the Great Commission. Jesus said, "Go and make disciples of all nations, baptizing them in the name of the Father and of the Son and of the Holy Spirit, and teaching them to obey everything I have commanded you. And surely I am with you always, to the very end of the age" (Matt. 28:19–20).

Just as your personal mission will be in harmony with your spiritual gifts, every church will express its mission in its own way. But if your church's mission is not some variation of the Great Commission, why does it exist? Jesus gave that charge to his disciples right before he ascended back to heaven. What could be more important than making disciples, baptizing them, and discipling them, with the knowledge that he is with us?

Cast Your Vision

Your vision is what the mission looks like in your particular situation. In your city or community, with your people, with your church's potential, with your opportunities, what does ministry look like? Visualize a picture of what the mission looks like as expressed through your unique circumstances.

If you cannot picture it, it isn't clear enough in your own mind. Alan Nelson compares casting a vision to a person guiding a group of people through a cave. As the guide, you are in front. You have the flashlight and it's up to you to shine the light so people can see the way. The people you are guiding have never been through the cave before. Without your guiding light, they may trip, make a wrong turn, or turn back out of fear. "A vision is a light that shows followers where to go. Do your job."[3]

Visionary Churches

Researcher George Barna observed that one of the key distinctions between churches that are growing and healthy and those that are stagnant or in decline is the existence of true vision for ministry.

Set Your Goals

Based on the vision you have for ministry in your location, it is absolutely essential that you set realistic, measureable goals. Without specific goals, you will never know if you are reaching your vision.

Paul Meyer makes an excellent point when he defines success as the "progressive realization of predetermined, worthwhile, personal goals."[4] He is speaking about individuals for whom the goals must be personal or there will be no incentive to achieve them. But the same is true for churches. If the goals do not relate to specific needs in the church or community, no one will be motivated to reach them.

Dreams

We grow by dreams. All big [individuals] are dreamers. They see things in the soft haze of a spring day, or in the red fire on a long winter's evening. Some of us let those great dreams die, but others nourish and protect them; nourish them through bad days until they bring them to the sunshine and light which comes always to those who sincerely hope that their dreams will come true.

—Woodrow Wilson

I particularly like Meyer's point about "progressive realization." Some goals take time, months, even years to achieve. But every goal can be broken down into bite-sized pieces. If you make progress on your goals today or this week, you are successful. It helps avoid discouragement when goals are stubborn and take longer to accomplish than you thought.

Putting deadlines on goals is essential. Otherwise they are too nebulous. But having said that, if you realize you are not going to accomplish your goals by the deadline, it doesn't mean you have bad goals. It means you may need to revise your timetable. If the goals are legitimate, keep after them.

Chart Your Progress

Let me show you how easy it is to chart your progress. Ask yourself these questions: "Did I make any progress toward reaching my goals today? Did we as a church make any progress toward reaching our goals today?" Now that's easy. You know what else is easy? Letting it slide. It's easy to become busy with the urgent and forget the important stuff, the things for which you have set goals. Resist the impulse to let it slide. Keep track.

Help your board learn to do this. Give progress reports at each board meeting. How far have you come? How much money has been raised toward the project? How many people have been won to Christ? How many people have used the church's food pantry? How many homeless people have been served? You get the idea.

Soon board members will expect a progress report. But that doesn't let them off the hook. They're not just there to watch you reach the goals. Involve them. They should have some assignment that makes them a vital part of reaching the goals. You may want to organize them into action teams, with each team responsible for some aspect of reaching the goal. Use your imagination.

Celebrate Your Victories

Obviously, when you reach a goal, you should celebrate. Have a party. If it's one of those "progressive realization" situations — you haven't reached the entire goal, but only a part — the celebration won't be as large as the one you will have when you've reached the big goal. But celebrate anyway.

Unfortunately, some of us are better at whining than we are at celebrating. We need to improve and learn to express our joy at making incremental progress.

Oiling the Wheels

Your achievements may not make the newspaper like the elderly man and his friends who crossed the ocean in a raft. But that doesn't mean your achievements are any less significant.

Every board is capable of making progress. First you have to cast a vision for your goals, and then design a plan to make them become a reality. Charting your progress along the way keeps both you and your board encouraged. Celebrating victories, even minor ones, will keep your projects infused with joy, a key element in oiling the wheels of progress.

Action Steps

1. Develop a chart showing your church's progress in the past ten years. Show such things as worship attendance, conversions, and baptisms. Before you can determine where you need to go, it is helpful to know where you have been and where you are.
2. Lead your church board through the process of developing mission and vision statements for your congregation.
3. Name five realistic, reachable goals your church could accomplish in the next year. How will you reach them? How will you keep track?

6

Initiative
Developing Long-Term Strategies

*Pastors who want long-term success need to
develop long-term strategies.*

I don't know why we even have church board meetings," Frank
said, stirring his coffee.

Jim stared back at him and said, "Don't you think it's important
to hear the reports every month? After all, we have to keep people
accountable, you know."

"Well, sure, but we know the treasurer is an honest man. I can't
imagine anyone questioning Stu's integrity. It isn't just that. I know
it's important to hear what the youth pastor has been doing and
how well the home Bible studies are getting along and all that. But
it seems like it's the same thing month after month. I just feel like,
as a church, we're spinning our wheels."

"In other words, we're doing a lot of good things, but we're
maintaining, rather than advancing?"

"Yeah, that's a good way to say it. We're maintaining. And
maybe that's all we can hope for. After all, these are pretty tough
days. As Christians, we're swimming upstream against the current

of our culture. So maybe we're fortunate to be holding our own. Yet I still feel that our pastor should be showing more initiative. Don't get me wrong; I love the guy. He gives great sermons, and he's a good counselor from what I hear. When my wife's mother was in the hospital, he was right there. A great source of comfort."

Frank sipped his coffee, and continued. "But where's our church going? I would just like to see the pastor put forth some sort of strategy for the future. Our attendance has been stagnant at about 220 for a couple of years now. Do we have any plans for significant outreach to the community? Does it always have to be this way? Or if we had a good strategy for outreach, could we really make a difference in the community around us?"

The Perils of Inaction

Frank has put his finger on something that every pastor must come to grips with sooner or later. Though he may not have used the same words, he sensed what Oswald Sanders said: "*To initiate* is an important function of the office of a leader. Some have more gift for conserving gains than for initiating new ventures; more gift for achieving order than for generating ardor. The true leader must have venturesomeness as well as vision. He [or she] must be an initiator rather than a mere conserver."[1]

Frank's pastor did well at managing the church, but was struggling to lead the church forward. The pastor had fallen into the trap of many who learn the hard way that doing things the right way is not the same as doing the right things. He was managing the church well and was a better conserver of gains than an initiator of new ventures. The church was stable, but it had settled for a comfortable routine rather than initiating great strategies for a bright future.

Why are some people brimming with initiative, while others seem to lack any resourcefulness at all?

Waiting for Someone Else to Get the Ball Rolling

I know people who are great at doing what needs to be done if someone will just tell them what to do. I think of the stereotypical picture of several government workers who are standing around a hole in the ground. One poor fellow is digging and throwing dirt for all he's worth, while the others are leaning on their shovels. Are they waiting for someone to come along and tell them what to do?

If we never learn the art of self-motivation, we will always achieve less than what God intended us to accomplish in life.

Having a Tendency to Procrastinate

Victor Kiam pointed out, "Procrastination is opportunity's natural assassin."[2] While we are waiting for the right opportunity, several pass right by

Self-Motivation

As a pastor, increased effectiveness may be only one motivational step away. It may be:

1. An *idea* away. Sometimes a new idea, insight, or way of doing things will spark new vision and action.
2. An *inspiration* away. Sometimes a word of encouragement, an inspiring model of an effective pastor, or a story of what is happening in another church sends people home with new energy.
3. An *enduement* away. Sometimes we need a new empowerment by God that may come through the prayers of others.
4. An *inspection* away. Sometimes accountability— knowing others are holding us to a course of action—is all that is needed to keep us focused on the task.

—Adapted from Ken Heer

Overcoming Procrastination

The wise man does at once
what the fool does finally.

—Baltasar Gracian

without our recognizing them. They die for lack of being seized and used.

Many people procrastinate out of fear. They are afraid that if they actually try something, they may fail, they may do it imperfectly, or someone may criticize their efforts. Whatever the fear, it paralyzes them from initiating action.

How sad if a pastor fails to seize the opportunities to accomplish something great for God because he or she is afraid of failing or afraid of criticism. Failure teaches us that we may have had the wrong approach or our timing may have been off a bit. But if we learn from the failure, we can get back in the game.

Finding Excuses Why Now Is Not a Good Time

A schoolboy near Monterrey, Mexico, took extreme action to skip school. He used superglue to bind his hand to his bed. When the press heard about this and interviewed his mother, she said that when she came to roust the boy out of bed before the opening of the spring semester, she found him calmly watching television, his hand firmly stuck to the bed. He said to her, "I didn't want to go to school because vacation was so much fun."[3]

Most adults would be too embarrassed to use such an excuse to avoid taking initiative. Yet some have become quite adept in finding excuses why they have not succeeded. George Washington Carver observed, "Ninety-nine percent of the failures come from people who have the habit of making excuses."[4] Unfortunately, those who are good at making excuses are seldom good at anything else. It's hard to excel at some legitimate endeavor if we excel at making excuses.

If the excuse-makers spent that same time and effort on taking initiative and grabbing an opportunity by the throat, they might discover the formula for success. However, as long as we continue making excuses, we can be sure that true achievement will elude us.

Unaware That Inaction Can Be Demoralizing

Failing to take initiative can actually be demoralizing. The person who constantly puts off getting started, delays taking action, and makes excuses for failing to move forward cannot be happy with his or her performance. Inaction leaves us with a vague sense of unfulfilled dreams that makes it hard to look at ourselves in the mirror. We know we are capable of greater things.

It's true that taking action involves risk. It would have been more comfortable not to put a man on the moon. The billions of dollars spent on the space program certainly could have been spent on other things. But when President Kennedy stood before a joint session of Congress in May of 1961, he said, "I believe this nation should commit itself to the goal, before this decade is out, of landing a man on the moon and returning him safely to Earth."[5] Such a goal was nearly unthinkable. But Kennedy said, "We choose to go to the moon in this decade and do the other things—*not* because they are easy, but because they are *hard*."[6]

That initiative brought out the best of our abilities and skills. It involved huge risk. But it paid huge dividends.

Excuses! Excuses!

The Bible has many examples of people who were slow to take initiative. When God spoke to Moses in the burning bush, the man who eventually led millions out of Egypt and through the wilderness stalled and stammered. In fact, "Moses pleaded with the LORD, 'O Lord, I'm not very good with words. I never have been, and I'm not now, even though you have spoken to me. I get tongue-tied, and my words get tangled'" (Ex. 4:10 NLT).

Leaders Who Stifle Potential

But God was not about to accept Moses' excuses. "The LORD asked Moses, 'Who makes a person's mouth? Who decides whether people speak or do not speak, hear or do not hear, see or do not see? Is it not I, the LORD? Now go! I will be with you as you speak, and I will instruct you in what to say'" (Ex. 4:11–12 NLT).

While God is not willing to accept our excuses, he is willing to help us overcome our hesitation when we are ready to cooperate with his program and take initiative.

The Lord had to overcome Gideon's objections too. This man who was threshing wheat in a winepress in the hope that the enemy would not discover him was just as reluctant as Moses. When God approached him about leading the people, he argued with the Lord. "'But Lord,' Gideon replied, 'how can I rescue Israel? My clan is the weakest in the whole tribe of Manasseh, and I am the least in my entire family!'" (Judg. 6:15 NLT).

And again, the Lord had an answer for his objections. "The LORD said to him, 'I will be with you. And you will destroy the Midianites as if you were fighting against one man'" (Judg. 6:16 NLT).

People Who Make Excuses

Jesus told a parable of a great banquet to be held at the end time. The host sent invitations to several who failed to seize the opportunity,

"But they all alike began to make excuses. The first said, 'I have just bought a field, and I must go and see it. Please excuse me.' Another said, 'I have just bought five yoke of oxen, and I'm on my way to try them out. Please excuse me.' Still another said, 'I just got married, so I can't come'" (Luke 14:18–20).

The fact is that the men in the parable did not simply miss an opportunity. The deeper truth is that they missed salvation because they believed their excuses more than they believed the Master.

Lessons for the Sluggard

The wise man wrote about those who were slow to take initiative. "The sluggard craves and gets nothing, but the desires of the diligent are fully satisfied" (Prov. 13:4). The diligent are those who have learned to take initiative. Like many people who know they should do better, the "sluggard craves." But craving does not accomplish anything unless it leads to action.

The diligent? Here's what the wise man said: "The plans of the diligent lead to profit as surely as haste leads to poverty" (Prov. 21:5).

Perhaps Solomon spoke most eloquently about initiative when he wrote about the ant: "Go to the ant, you sluggard; consider its ways and be wise! It has no commander, no overseer or ruler, yet it stores its provisions in summer and gathers its food at harvest. How long will you lie there, you sluggard? When will you get up from your sleep? A little sleep, a little slumber, a little folding of the hands to rest—and poverty will come on you like a bandit and scarcity like an armed man" (Prov. 6:6–11).

Solomon's words scorch us! In essence he said, "Look down from your lofty height as a human being, a giant compared to an ant, and learn from the ways of this tiny insect." And what do we learn?

- They don't need some superintendent over them.
- They get the essentials done first.
- They work ahead of time so they can relax later.
- They do it all without fanfare or applause.[7]

With customary brilliance, the wise man succinctly stated how taking initiative and fulfilling a dream satisfies our deepest longing. "Hope deferred makes the heart sick, but a longing fulfilled is a tree of life. . . . A longing fulfilled is sweet to the soul" (Prov. 13:12, 19).

Human beings are unique in our abilities to think, reason, plan, and take initiative. Animals can't do it. The strongest horse cannot formulate a plan. Chickens, ducks, and birds of the air steadfastly refuse. They may operate by instinct, such as we see them do when they build nests. But proposing a strategy? That ability belongs to human beings.

Solomon said, "To man belongs the plans of the heart" (Prov. 16:1), emphasizing our uniqueness among the creatures God created. But lest we become too great in our own eyes, he added, "Commit to the LORD whatever you do, and your plans will succeed" (Prov. 16:3).

Taking Initiative

Initiative is not about avoiding risk; it's about taking action. Initiative is not about waiting for someone to tell you what to do; it's about being a self-starter. It's not about wondering what to do; it's about making decisions.

Colin Powell served as chairman of the Joint Chiefs of Staff during the Gulf War when George H. W. Bush was president, and then a secretary of state when George W. Bush was president. He knew something about initiative when he said:

> Good leaders don't wait for official blessing to try things out. They're prudent, not reckless. But they also realize a fact of life in most organizations: if you ask enough people for permission, you'll inevitably come up against someone who believes his job is to say "no." So the moral is, don't ask. Less effective middle managers endorsed the sentiment, "If I haven't explicitly been told 'yes,' I can't do it," whereas the good ones believed, "If I haven't explicitly been told 'no,' I can." There's a world of difference between these two points of view.[8]

I have known pastors who are afraid to make a decision without asking their church board. Obviously, a pastor has to know what his or her limits are, but to be paralyzed for fear of overstepping one's authority is an initiative killer. Most boards are happy when a pastor is confident enough to take initiative. To apply Powell's principle, sensible pastors are "prudent, not reckless." But neither are they paralyzed.

Action

An African proverb captures the idea of action very well: Every morning in Africa, a gazelle wakes up. It knows that it must run faster than the fastest lion or it will be killed. Every morning a lion wakes up. It knows that it must outrun the slowest gazelle or it will starve to death. It doesn't matter whether you are a lion or a gazelle: When the sun comes up you had better be running.

Taking the First Step

Taking initiative begins with taking the first step. You have to begin somewhere. If you know where you are now, the next question is: "Where do we go from here?" Then take the first step.

I read somewhere about two women who lived on the bayou in Louisiana. One woman complained constantly. She griped about life on the bayou. She groused about being stuck in a small house and about being poor. Day in and day out, she grumbled that nobody had it as bad as she did. Finally, her neighbor had enough.

"Listen, girl," she began, "if you don't like it here, go somewhere else. The bayou empties into the creek, the creek runs into the river, the river flows to the gulf, and they tell me the gulf connects to the ocean. So what I'm telling you, sister, is this: from the bayou, you can go anywhere you want. Stop complainin'!"

She was right. But what she said to her carping neighbor could be said to all of us. Starting from where you live, you can go anywhere. That doesn't mean you should move. There are destinations of the mind and spirit that need to be reached as much as geographical destinations. Where does your church need to go? What does your congregation need to accomplish? Take the first step. From where you are, you can go anywhere and reach any goal.

Determining a New Direction

How do you determine what direction you should move? Consider this: What are your problems, projects, and possibilities? What are your options and opportunities? What are the dreams you are dreaming, decisions you are facing, or dilemmas you are encountering?

As you consider these questions, you will find the direction to begin your initiative. It may be as simple as asking yourself, "What needs to be done?"

Life does not have to be rocket science. It may be as simple as finding a need and filling it or finding a hurt and healing it. But you have to get up out of your chair and get to work. Take initiative.

Charles Schwab said, "The difference between getting somewhere and nowhere is the courage to make an early start. The fellow who sits still and does just what he is told will never be told to do big things."[9]

Learning to Spot Opportunities

Opportunities are the breeding ground for initiative. The problem is that we don't always see them as such. We see them as problems, inconveniences, detours, or delays. But every time you meet someone new, you have an opportunity. Every time you face a problem, you are meeting an opportunity in disguise. Every time someone criticizes you, you have an enormous opportunity.

Andy Stanley says, "Our tendency is to pray for miracles. But in most situations, it is more appropriate to pray for opportunities. More than likely you need an opportunity rather than something supernatural."[10] So learn to think differently. Instead of obstacles, learn to see opportunities. Instead of problems, think possibilities. Instead of adversity, think creativity; and your mind begins to envision opportunities. It doesn't mean the obstacles, problems, and adversities are not real. They are very real. But refusing to allow them to sidetrack you permanently allows your mind to envision new ways of dealing with them. It enables you to turn a stumbling block into a stepping stone.

Strategies for Growth

As important as it is to get started, we can't stop there. The adage that reminds us, "Beginning is half-done," is meant to encourage us to get started. The problem is when we fail to continue, it is still true: We're only half done.

Long-Term Strategies

Many good beginnings have failed to yield positive fruit because they died for lack of a strategic plan. Mark Victor Hansen pointed out that "Walt Disney and R. Buckminster Fuller [who invented many things, most notably the geodesic dome] had 50 year plans." Then he asked the poignant question: "Do you?"[11]

I admit only a few pastors ever stay at their churches for fifty years. But that does not keep us from developing a long-term strategy. One of my colleagues challenged his church to reach one thousand in attendance when they were running half that number. He was called by his denomination to take a position as district superintendent before the church achieved that goal. A year after he left, a leading layman called him and said, "Pastor, I know that one of your goals was to reach one thousand in attendance. I just wanted you to know, we reached it."

Would the church have accomplished that goal if my friend had not planted the seed? Who knows? Not to take anything away from his successor who continued the good work my colleague had begun, but once a seed is planted, it will surely grow given enough encouragement.

What are some areas in which you can strategize and lead your board to think in terms of long-range plans? If fifty years sounds too ambitious, surely every church should think in terms of where they would like to be in five years or ten years. Such plans would involve thinking in terms of ministering to greater numbers of people, which should result in greater financial resources. Larger numbers of people will likely necessitate expanded facilities, perhaps even relocation. Larger numbers of people will represent more workers for kingdom interests.

Strategies for Growth

Write down your ideas. If your church experienced a net gain of 5 percent per year, where will you be in five to ten years? What if you experience a 10 percent annual gain? What kinds of facilities would you need for children's ministries? For youth ministries? Would your worship space be adequate? What kind of impact could you make on your community?

Don't be ashamed of thinking in terms of numbers. Numbers aren't everything, but they are easy to count. They help us know where we are and where we want to go. We count people because people count, especially in God's eyes, and in our eyes too.

Purpose

No individual has any right to come into the world and go out of it without leaving behind him distinct and legitimate reasons for having passed through it.

—George Washington Carver

A simple, clear statement of purpose will form a good foundation for strategic thinking. Something as simple as this: Our purpose is to bring people to Christ, build them up in Christ, and enlist them in service for Christ. If you believe that, and if it is your purpose, what kinds of plans should you make?

Strategies for Meeting Needs

Part of your strategic thinking should involve meeting the needs of people. What are the needs of the people in your community? Yes, every community has people who need Christ. But what can you do for people that will let them know you care? Should you start a food bank? Would it make sense in your community to start an after-school program for kids? How could you partner with the school near your church? What about a tutoring program for students who are having difficulty?

Strategies for Reaching and Involving More People

How effective are your people at sharing their faith? What can you do to increase their effectiveness in reaching others? A course in friendship evangelism might be a good place to start. Developing consistent ways to encourage your people to invite their unchurched friends can bring more people into the fold.

Reaching New People

It is easier to plan for the known than the unknown. It is easier to plan for yesterday than for tomorrow. These two temptations encourage leaders to attempt to respond to the agendas and priorities of today's mature members rather than to anticipate the preferences of people we have never met.

—Lyle E. Schaller

Think strategically about how you can welcome newcomers more effectively. What percentage of first-time visitors return for a second visit? A third visit? Do you have any way of tracking this information? What are you doing to connect newcomers to established attendees? Strategize about ways to integrate newcomers into the life of your church.

Another part of your strategic thinking should determine how to involve more of your parishioners in ministry. Some church growth experts tell us that at least 50 percent of the people in growing churches are involved in some form of service.[12] What percentage of your people are involved in some form of ministry at least once a month?

Strategies for Developing Leaders

Growing churches are constantly developing more leaders. What is happening in your church to develop more and better leaders? What should be happening? What if the leader of every current ministry in your church recruited an apprentice to work alongside him or her? In a matter of time, you can double the number of leaders. You can only have as many ministries as you have people to lead them.

Are you beginning to get the idea of strategizing about anything and everything that can help your church be more effective? Your board should be on the cutting edge of these strategic plans. As Bobb Biehl says, "A clear dream energizes your plans. And a clear plan unlocks your dreams."[13]

A Different Board Meeting

"Wow! What happened to our pastor?" Frank exclaimed as he and Jim met for their usual Wednesday morning coffee. "That board meeting last night was awesome!"

"I know! What Pastor said about strategic planning made a lot of sense. Leading us through the discussion of determining a simple purpose statement really helped to clarify why we exist as a church!"

"Right! I mean, we all know we're supposed to reach people for Christ, but to begin thinking in terms of why we do it and then to see how that helps us form our strategy for the future makes so much sense."

"You know, I believe there's hope for our church after all. In fact, I can't wait until next month's board meeting as we continue thinking and planning for the future!"

Frank and Jim's eagerness over the direction of their church is no accident. Thinking strategically energizes people. It gets them off their plateau and helps them to think about growth. It rouses them from their doldrums and inspires them to think about the possibilities. What will God do if we pray and make plans with his values in view?

Action Steps

1. How good is your board at strategizing? Write down three ways you can help them improve.
2. In honest self-appraisal, what have you been procrastinating about? Write a positive declaration of when you will accomplish the object of your procrastination.
3. What first steps will you take that will establish your initiative?

7

RETREATS
CONDUCTING STRATEGIC
PLANNING GETAWAYS

*A well-planned retreat can help a board to
engage in strategic planning.*

O h, no, not another retreat," Susan lamented as she left the
board room.

Janice, a new board member, said, "I thought a retreat sounded
like it might be a great experience."

"Oh, it's just that our former pastor used to have these annual
retreats that either bored us to death or made us feel foolish with
all the wacky games he forced us to play. He used to be a youth
pastor, and I don't think he ever got over his love for seeing
people do ridiculous things. But none of us were fourteen, and
his antics drove me up the wall. When he wasn't boring us with
his interminable lectures, that is."

As they exited the building, Janice said, "Well, in the church
we used to attend, retreats were well-planned and interesting. We
really got into some significant strategic planning, and it gave us
time to deal with issues we just didn't have time for in regular
board meetings."

"That sounds ideal, but I'm afraid I'm gun shy, after what our former pastor put us through."

"I can understand, but I think we ought to give our new pastor a chance. His background and experience are different. At least we ought to attend the retreat with an open mind. Maybe this one will be refreshingly different than the ones you're used to."

"Of course I'll be there. But I must admit, I'm a doubting Thomas. I'll believe it when I see it."

Planning

The reason why most people face the future with apprehension instead of anticipation is because they don't have it well designed.

—Jim Rohn

Susan and Janice are both right, given their previous experiences. People who have had bad experiences with board retreats would be happy never to attend another one. But board members who have attended well-planned, effective retreats know their value and realize they can be effective in moving the church board forward.

How to Kill a Retreat

With a little effort, anyone can kill a retreat and ensure that board members won't ever want to participate again. Here, with tongue firmly planted in cheek, are some surefire ways to doom a retreat.

Don't Worry about Planning

Retreats are meant to help people relax, right? Too much planning can kill anything. Over preparation will make you a nervous wreck. You'll enter into the experience with frazzled nerves and a cranky disposition. Relax. It will all work out!

Too much planning stifles creativity, right? Just bring people together and let it happen.

Plan for an Inflexible Time Schedule

If spontaneity is not your thing, consider developing a time schedule that completely eliminates it. Give people a chance, and they'll hijack your retreat. You know how some people are control freaks! Don't allow any wiggle room in your schedule, or somebody will come up with an off-the-wall idea that could sidetrack the whole weekend.

Don't Ask for Anyone's Input into the Planning and Format of the Retreat

You know what you want better than anyone else does. After all, as the pastor, who is responsible for running the church? Your laypeople are busy and have their own lives to think about. They probably don't have time to plan the retreat anyway. Besides, if you relinquish control of the planning, there's no telling what direction the retreat might take. You know the old saying, "If you want something done right, do it yourself."

Make the Format One of Lecture with No Feedback

Since you know the direction you want the church to take, who better to provide the major input than you? Besides, if you ask an outside resource person to come and present something to the board, that could run into a lot of money for honoraria, travel expenses, and lodging. The church is paying you anyway, so go ahead and plan all the lectures yourself and give them in your own unique style.

Be Sure the Retreat Is Irrelevant to the Real Needs of the Church

A retreat, by definition, is a getaway, right? So you don't want to make the content too heavy. Besides, some of the issues the church is facing are pretty heavy. If you get into that stuff, it could cause a lot of disagreement, controversy, and ill will that you really can't afford. Better keep the content light and avoid any issues that might cause division. It's important to keep the unity of the church, right?

Don't Give Any Time for Fellowship or Small Group Interaction

I hate to beat a dead horse, but you know how some people like to take over. If you break into small groups for any kind of inter-action, some people will talk too much, dominate the group, or upset the other members. And it will do more harm than good in the long run. Keeping everyone together and minimizing time for interaction is the best way to avoid controversy.

Relevance

We cannot afford to be irrelevant. There is too much at stake. The lost are all around us looking for direction. It's up to us to make sure they can find it.

—Charles Nieman

Plan to Tackle Far More Topics Than You Can Reasonably Address

If you change the subject frequently, it will keep people from becoming bored. After all, it's important to keep things moving, right? Fill your agenda with plenty of topics. That way you won't have to plan too much to say on any one topic, and that should help ease your preparation time. Too few topics could bog things down in heavy discussion and debate.

Make Your Schedule Full of Routine Tasks and Trivia

Some might argue that routine tasks and trivia could easily be accomplished in a regular board meeting. But at the same time, why waste the board's time when these things really need to be done. The secretary's report, the treasurer's report, and giving each ministry leader time to give an update on their activities will help fill time. Once again, this cuts down on your preparation.

Cut Off Any Idea That Arises, No Matter How Significant It Might Be

We're back to this idea of spontaneity. It can kill you, sidetrack you, bore people to death, and cause you to lose the focus you have worked so hard to create. People can come up with the weirdest ideas when they are turned loose and allowed to ask any question or bring up any topic. What if you haven't had time to prepare an answer? That could be embarrassing.

Be Sure to Have the Retreat in a Remote Location

If you can get a good price for the use of cabins at the retreat center fifteen miles from Podunk City, why not go for it? You can save the church some money by having it in a place that is a little hard to get to. Anyway, everybody has a GPS now, right? How hard can it be to find the place. And meals? No need to go overboard. Take several loaves of bread and some cold cuts. It's just one weekend, after all. Nobody needs to expect culinary delights on a retreat.

Seriously . . .

Hopefully, you caught the statement early on that these suggestions are presented tongue in cheek. Obviously, these are the things to *not* do if you want people to look forward to the next board retreat.

A Brief Retreat

Jesus knew the value of a retreat. He said to his disciples on one occasion, "Come with me by yourselves to a quiet place and get some rest" (Mark 6:31). This is not something to which the masses were invited. It was a time just for Jesus and his disciples to spend alone.

What were the circumstances that led to Jesus' desire for a retreat? Three momentous events preceded this effort at getting away with the disciples.

Stresses That Call for a Retreat

First, Jesus had gone back to his hometown of Nazareth for a visit. One might think he would receive a hero's welcome since he had been teaching and healing in Capernaum about twenty miles away. On the Sabbath, as was his custom, he began to teach in the synagogue, evoking amazement among the people who heard him. Yet the amazement was full of skepticism rather than faith. In fact, "they took offense at him" (Mark 6:3).

It was this reaction that prompted Jesus to say, "Only in his hometown, among his relatives, and in his own house is a prophet without honor" (Mark 6:4). The Messiah, who had

Give It Your Best

Whether in planning board retreats or whatever you are doing, ask yourself the questions suggested by Vaughn McLaughlin: "If your church were to leave the community you're in, what impact would it have? Would they miss you? Would they weep?" These will remind you that whatever you do, you must give it your best. Eternal values are at stake.

healed so many in Capernaum, could heal very few in Nazareth, and "he was amazed at their lack of faith" (Mark 6:6). On only one other occasion does the Scripture tell us Jesus was amazed—and that was in the case of the centurion's faith (Luke 7:9). In the latter story, Jesus was amazed at the strength of the man's faith, and in the former, he was amazed at the lack of the people's faith.

So this disappointing response from his townspeople and relatives formed the first in a series of momentous events.

The second event involved the sending out of the Twelve on a preaching and healing mission. Having observed his teaching, preaching, and healing, they were now ready to become missionaries themselves. In fact, Mark 6:30 calls them apostles, which means a person who is sent on an errand or mission, hence, a missionary.

Their mission was successful as they "preached that people should repent" and "drove out many demons and anointed many sick people with oil and healed them" (Mark 6:12–13). Returning from that experience, they "reported to [Jesus] all they had done and taught" (Mark 6:30). Mark added the detail that they were so busy "they did not even have a chance to eat" (Mark 6:31).

The third event preceding the retreat was the death of John the Baptist. In his forthright way, John had criticized King Herod for marrying Herodias, who had been married to Herod's brother Philip. John told him point-blank, "It is not lawful for you to have your brother's wife" (Mark 6:18).

Although John criticized Herod, the king protected him because he knew John was a holy man. He did not always understand John, but he paid attention to him. Herodias, on the other hand, hated John and wanted to kill him. She saw her opportunity when her daughter danced for the king and he offered her anything she wanted, up to half his kingdom. Herodias advised her daughter to ask for the head of John the Baptist. Although the king did not want to grant her request, his guests had heard him make the offer. So he had John executed.

Jesus held John in high esteem. On one occasion Jesus had said, "I tell you the truth: Among those born of women there has not risen anyone greater than John the Baptist" (Matt. 11:11).

When you add up these three events—the disappointing reception in Nazareth, the excitement of the disciples in returning from their preaching mission, and the sadness at the death of John the Baptist—it was emotionally and physically time for a retreat.

Times of Spiritual Renewal

Someone might argue the type of retreat Jesus and the disciples needed was not the same kind of retreat we are talking about in this chapter. Yet David McKenna asserts, regarding this incident, that it was a time for "personal privacy, which Jesus cherishes for times of spiritual renewal and teaching seminars."[1]

Their retreat was short-lived. The trip across the lake to find a quiet place was only four miles. And those who ran around the north end of the lake made good enough time to welcome them on the other shore.

And that was the extent of their retreat, because when they arrived on the opposite shore and Jesus saw a large crowd, "he had compassion on them, because they were like sheep without a shepherd. So he began teaching them many things" (Mark 6:34).

Enough Time for a Retreat

What could one accomplish in a two-hour retreat? Did Jesus try to teach them on the short voyage across the lake? If so, what did he teach them? They had already done their immediate debriefing about their mission before they took the voyage. Did he ask them to go into greater detail? Did he ask them what they learned? What they would do differently on the next mission? Did he ask about any converts? What kinds of healing took place during their mission?

Such questions can be highly instructive as people debrief, hear others talk, and gain insights from others' experiences. Did Jesus give a mini lecture, building on their experiences? Did he affirm them for their work? We will never know what occurred on the voyage across the lake, but I doubt if Jesus wasted time.

Retreating on Purpose

For board retreats to be instructive, practical, and worthwhile, it takes considerable planning. For one thing, what kind of retreat should it be? Stephen Tweed, in his work with not-for-profit health-care organizations, has identified four different types of retreats.[2] The principles are transferable to working with church boards. The type you use depends on what you want to accomplish.

Trends Retreat

If you feel that your board is out of touch with what is happening in the church world, particularly with highly successful churches, you can bring in a resource person to speak about the subject. You might be able to tell the board the same things a resource person would share, but because the resource person is an outsider, he or she lends an air of impartiality and credibility. The pastor of a church that is excelling in the kind of outreach or other ministry that you want your board to know about may be an ideal person to speak to your lay leaders. If the pastor can bring along a couple laypersons who can speak about what is happening in their church, so much the better.

A trends retreat is a way to inform your board, expand their horizons, and increase their understanding. Our vision is often limited because we don't know of any concrete examples. It's easy for people to think, "We've never done it that way before." But if you or a resource person can show that it is being done somewhere else, at least it creates the possibility that things could change for the better in your community.

Visioning Retreat

A pastor may have a vision for where he or she wants the church to go or what he or she wants the church to do. But the board may not have bought into that vision yet. You may be able to "sell" them on the vision by presenting it at a regular board meeting. But a visioning retreat provides a great opportunity not only to present a vision, but to interact about it and achieve buy-in.

It does take skill and patience to lead board members through a visioning process, have them talk about their ideas for the future, and allow them to shape the future. Again, a resource person may be able to do this more effectively than the pastor can. However, if you already have a strong sense of what the preferred future should be, you're better off to lead your own retreat.

Be aware, the end result may or may not look exactly like your personal vision. However, a skillful pastor can weave enough ideas into the discussion that the shared vision is one that everyone can embrace.

Remember, the important outcome is not the precise vision, but the fact that your opinion leaders embrace it and that it will move the church toward the desired outcomes.

Refocusing Retreat

As Tweed observes, "It's easy for board and staff to become distracted, diluted, and out of focus."[3] A retreat away from familiar surroundings can bring the thoughts, actions, and resources of the group back into focus in order to keep on track. The constant struggle in any organization is to keep the main thing the main thing.

Refocusing is reminding ourselves what is really important and committing ourselves to seek a few things, denying the many that would slow us down and divert our energies. As Thomas Carlyle said, "The weakest living creature, by concentrating his powers on a single object, can accomplish something; whereas the strongest, by dispersing his over many, may fail to accomplish anything."[4]

When your church is failing to move together in one direction, a refocusing retreat may be just what you need.

The Pastor's Role in Vision

Someone asked management expert Peter Drucker, "Besides preaching, how can a pastor work to implement vision?" He answered, "When you look at well-run organizations, you see that the top people sit in on personnel decisions, even at fairly low levels. . . . Part of the leader's job is to set the spirit of the organization. That doesn't mean simply to lay out policy and plans, but to exemplify them, to pay personal attention to the areas where the vision is being worked out."

Leadership Retreat

A leadership retreat can be an excellent way to impart leadership skills to your board. It can be a way of improving communication between board and staff. It can clarify expectations and understanding about the respective roles of board members, pastoral staff, and church staff.

A leadership retreat provides an excellent opportunity to build greater teamwork into the life of the board. A devotional period that focuses on being united under the lordship of Jesus Christ can set the tone for a retreat that deepens the board spiritually. A leadership retreat can also help develop lay leaders who have what Tom Phillips calls, "Nike hearts." They are people who are not satisfied simply to plan a great future, they want to "just do it!"[5]

A leadership retreat also provides the opportunity to communicate attitudes to help board members remain positive about the future after they have gone home from the retreat. Tennis champion Chris Evert said, "The thing that separates good players from great ones is mental attitude. It might only make a difference of two or three points in the entire match, but how you play those key points often makes the difference between winning and losing. If the mind is strong, you can do almost anything you want."[6]

If you can instill positive principles and cultivate positive attitudes during a board retreat, you can send your board members home with enough enthusiasm to charge hell with a water pistol!

Planning Your Strategy

A board retreat can be extremely useful for strategic planning. Time away, whether it is half a day, a full day, a day and a half, or an entire weekend, gives you time to devote to the process of strategic planning that you simply do not have in your regular monthly meetings. A strategic planning retreat may involve elements of the four types of retreats just named. Part of your retreat time may be used to introduce current trends. An effective retreat may stretch the vision of your group. One desired outcome of the retreat may be to refocus your board members and bring them on task as far as the mission and vision of the church are concerned. Certainly, leadership development is a part of strategic planning.

Here are some other key elements you will want to include as you plan and implement your retreat.

Establish an Agenda

Know what you want to accomplish and the steps you need to take to arrive at your desired outcome. Think through the process carefully. When your board arrives at the retreat site, members may still be wound tightly because of the stressful schedules they have been keeping. Therefore, design your agenda so it takes them through a process of unwinding before you organize them to focus on the business at hand.

Include Devotions

You may want to include a passage of Scripture that talks about the importance of retreating, pulling aside for awhile, taking intentional time to draw close to the Lord and others. Cite Scriptures that reinforce the theme you are using for your retreat. While we can learn from business models, this is the Lord's work. So taking time for Scripture and prayer is not just a habitual exercise; it is recognizing the spiritual dimension of what we do for Christ and his church.

Present the Topic for the Retreat[7]

What is it you need to plan? What aspect of the church's work needs the focus of the group's strategic thinking and planning? Be sure that your topic fits within the scope of mission, vision, and values.

Mission. Mission is the overall goal, and it never changes. This is the big-picture statement that answers the question: "Why are we here?" In fact, many mission statements begin with the words: "We exist in order to . . ."

Vision. Vision provides focus for what the church will become or accomplish in this particular place at this particular time. Vision should be local, specific, and inspiring. For example, your church might declare, "Our vision is to reach every home in this community with the gospel of Jesus Christ."

Values. Values are the nonnegotiable characteristics of a church, its heart and soul. They guide leaders and enable them to say the crucial word *no*. If a new project is proposed, it must pass through the grid of values to determine whether it fits the church's identity and purpose. If it will, then it moves to the next level of planning. If it does not match the church's values, it gets the big N-O.

Strategy. Strategy is the plan for accomplishing the vision. It incorporates all relevant considerations in a way that provides the most efficient means of getting the job done. An effective strategy includes strategic objectives, intermediate and long-term plans that advance the vision.

Goals. Goals represent what the organization desires to accomplish within a certain time frame. Goals must be specific, measurable, and dated. A church's goal might be to win twenty-five people to Christ within one year. Goals become the objective criteria for measuring effectiveness and ultimately, progress.

Know your mission. See your vision clearly. Communicate both effectively, and you will succeed.

Consider Storyboarding

Storyboarding is a process of telling a story or diagramming a process with the use of pictures, diagrams, and other visuals. It was first used by the Walt Disney Studios in the 1930s. The first complete storyboards were created for the 1933 Disney production of *Three Little Pigs*. The process has been used with many kinds of storytelling, *Gone with the Wind* being the first full-length motion picture to be completely storyboarded.[8]

> **Strategic Planning**
>
> The wise man bridges the gap by laying out the path by means of which he can get from where he is to where he wants to go.
>
> —John Pierpont Morgan

As it relates to your retreat, participants may use index cards, push pins, felt pens, and foam boards as tools in the process. The purpose is to take creative ideas and visualize them. It helps to capture the results of in-depth discussions. It also gets people involved in a hands-on effort to make their thoughts come alive.

Document the Results

Be sure to appoint someone to take notes on the meeting as a way of conserving the fruit of your discussion and planning. Or take the items created in the storyboarding process. The results could be transferred to a computer later. But documenting the results will enable you to remember your plans. You may want to refer to them at some future time.

A Retreat That Advanced

"I'm so glad we went on the retreat," Susan said after she and Janice ordered their sandwiches. Sitting at the table and sipping their soft drinks, they laughed about some of the things they had done on their board retreat the previous weekend.

"I'm glad I went too," Janice said. "The pastor provided some creative ways to stimulate our thinking. And I loved the storyboarding process. Wasn't that fun?"

Susan laughed. "Yes, my stick figures would never win a prize for art, but I guess they helped tell the story."

"You know, another thing I appreciated was the way the pastor distinguished between vision, mission, values, and goals. I have heard people toss those words around for a long time, but this weekend was the first time I saw the connection between them so clearly."

"I agree," said Susan. "And I've changed my mind about retreats. I can't wait for the next one."

Action Steps

1. Write down three areas of your church's ministry that could profit from strategic planning.
2. Of the four (or five, if you include strategic planning as a fifth option) types of retreats mentioned in this chapter, which is the most needed by your board?
3. Schedule a weekend to conduct a retreat with your board. Begin brainstorming with some key leaders as to what you want to accomplish.

8

CONFLICT
MANAGING CLASHING OPINIONS AND PERSONALITIES

A wise pastor learns to manage conflict proactively.

I don't think we should do anything without giving the congregation a chance to give the money," Cindy said, folding her arms.

"But the district has offered to loan us the money, interest free," Bob countered. "The people have already pledged through our Capital Stewardship Campaign, some of them sacrificially. So I hate to see us make another appeal this soon."

"Bob is right," Tom added, from the other end of the table. "If we accept the district's offer now, we can finish our remodeling project without further delay. The congregation has put up with the mess and the inconvenience for several weeks now. I say it's time to get it done!'"

"I hear you," Cindy responded, "but as board members, we're supposed to be the spiritual leaders of the church. We have been praying for God to supply this need and I think we should give him a chance to meet the need, instead of borrowing the money."

"But, Cindy, listen to reason," Bob said. "God has answered our prayers—and it's interest free! We can pay it back as the people continue to pay their pledges."

"We said we weren't going to borrow the money!" Cindy said, clenching her teeth.

"But if it's interest free, that's not the same thing!"

From his seat at the chairman's end of the table, Pastor Ken prayed silently, "Dear Lord, give me wisdom to moderate this issue. Unless you intervene, someone is going to walk out of this meeting very unhappy. Maybe everyone will, if we're deadlocked."

We can all identify with Pastor Ken's prayer for wisdom. As wonderful as our brothers and sisters in Christ are, they are human and don't always see eye to eye. It's not just that one side is right and the other is wrong. It's a difference of opinion, priorities, and viewpoints.

Just as a small spark can start a forest fire, so issues like this can roar out of proportion until they destroy fellowship, stall momentum, divide congregations, and even ruin churches.

The Time Is Ripe for Conflict

Believe it or not, there are certain times—almost predictable—when problems are likely to occur in the life of a church.

Capital Stewardship Campaign

During a capital stewardship campaign, regardless of the reason a church wants to raise money, conflict may arise. In many such campaigns, outside consultants will advise the church leadership to train lay volunteers to visit the constituents in their homes and share with them the purpose of the campaign, answer questions, and ask for prayer requests. It is during some of these visits that people may begin to complain about the pastor, the church staff, or some program of the church that does not suit them. Since people do not normally have a formal way of registering complaints, they may use such visits to vent.

However, I have known of campaigns during which the people genuinely appreciated their fellow lay members' visits and the opportunity to share their needs with someone who cares.

The campaign itself is likely to draw some opposition because constituents are asked to step up and make a commitment, often a sacrificial one. Those less committed—or less convinced—may use this opportunity to criticize. Others may slip quietly out the back door and start attending a church that does not require that level of commitment.

When Attendance Decreases

Few churches enjoy a constant increase in attendance year after year. Almost all churches eventually experience a plateau, and most suffer losses at times. When attendance drops, people may look around and wonder where their friends are. Sometimes the loss is about job change or a downturn in the economy. Even if the circumstances are beyond control, the pastor may receive criticism for the losses.

If people leave the church because of dissatisfaction and if they are vocal about their reasons, negativity can spread, and so can its accompanying blame and gloom. Others may join the cause and play the blame game. Conflict is the result and it may grow.

When Attendance Increases

Ironically, conflict may also arise when attendance increases. Sister Sarah can't sit in her regular pew anymore because some new person has had the audacity to sit there. New people may bring new talent, fresh skills, and experiences that they are eager to put to use. Incumbents may feel their power and influence slipping away and resent the newcomers.

As churches grow, they require a different kind of organization. A church of 150 cannot function the same way a church of fifty can. Suddenly, long-time members of the church don't know everybody who is attending. The family feeling isn't the same as it used to be. Strangers are sitting in the pews and milling in the foyer. Veterans may feel their comfort level declining in direct proportion to the growing attendance.

When Staffing Changes Occur

When a pastor resigns and the congregation is faced with choosing a new leader, conflict can creep into the church. Polity varies from one denomination to another, but in churches that interview candidates and choose their next pastor, lay leaders can struggle for dominance. Disagreements may arise as to what kind of pastor is needed. One group may feel that their viewpoint is not being heard as readily as another group's opinion. Similar conflict can arise if a popular staff member leaves.

Even though such changes are inevitable, a lead pastor can be blamed for the loss by board members and others who are insensitive to the realities of church life. Such changes provide a congregation with opportunities to mature; they also provide opportunities for conflict.

When a Change in Worship Style Occurs

Who hasn't heard one horror story after another about the casualties of the worship wars? A pastor wants to lead his or her congregation from a totally traditional worship style to a more contemporary one. I have known churches where long-time members walked out, almost en masse, because a new pastor made such changes too abruptly.

When changes are made in such a way that they seem arbitrary, with little input from the congregation, without explanation and/or without sensitivity, they nearly always result in conflict. Some pastors take the attitude, "So what? It's time to change! Let 'em leave, and we'll just get more people who like the new style."

Other pastors approach changes with greater sensitivity, make changes gradually, refuse to throw out the proverbial baby with the bath water, and bring everyone along together. It takes longer but results in greater unity and fewer casualties.

Intense, Frequent Conflict

When conflict is intense and frequent, God's people stop growing spiritually, stop loving one another, and stop reaching out to new people with the life-changing gift of Christ. When conflict is minimal, mission and ministry can become maximal.

—Herb Miller

During a Building Program

Closely related to the stewardship campaign is the building program. A new building or even a major remodeling project can cause a great deal of inconvenience to a congregation. For a period of time, as in this chapter's opening story, church members are subjected to dust and dirt. Worship and educational space may have to be rearranged for the duration of the project. Unless the leadership keeps a clear picture of the desired result before the congregation, people grow restless and weary. Then if delays result, nerves wear thin and conflict ensues.

Unfortunately, at the end of many building programs, pastors leave. They become so war-torn and weary by the end of the project they do not have the energy to continue and enjoy the fruits of their labors. Sometimes it just seems easier to leave and start over again somewhere else.

Conflict among Friends

A road trip with a few of your closest friends—sounds like a pleasant way to spend an afternoon. Not for this group. Their journey led to an argument about who was the greatest among them.

Who Is the Greatest?

To be fair, tensions had been running high. Perhaps it all started when Jesus took Peter, James, and John with him up to Mount Hermon, where he was transfigured before them. It was an awesome experience for those three, but why those three? Perhaps the others wondered why Peter, James, and John were treated to a special experience while the others were left to deal with a boy possessed by an evil spirit. The spirit often threw the boy into the fire or water and caused him to convulse, fall to the ground, roll around, and foam at the mouth.

To add insult to injury, the disciples could not cast out the demon. Further, the whole incident led to an argument with the teachers of the law. These experts were asking questions and putting pressure on the disciples who were sincere, but unschooled.

Their training was simply not on a par with the teachers of the law. This was the scene Jesus saw when he and the three disciples descended from the Mount of Transfiguration.

Jesus rebuked the evil spirit and it came out of the boy, but not before it shrieked and violently convulsed the boy. And although the evil spirit fled, it left the boy so limp that some wondered if he was dead. Jesus, however, lifted him to his feet and restored him to health.

When the disciples, frustrated over their inability to cast out the demon, asked Jesus about it, he told them that such things could only come about by prayer. So not only were they incapable of casting out demons, they could have inferred that Jesus meant they were also spiritually deficient. And although the disciples did not fully understand, Jesus predicted his death as they walked along, which only made things feel gloomier.

When they arrived in Capernaum and finally had a chance to sit down and regroup, Jesus asked them an embarrassing question: "What were you arguing about on the road?" They did not answer him because "they had argued about who was the greatest" (Mark 9:33–34).

Tensions and misunderstandings notwithstanding, it is a sad commentary on human nature. We might credit the disciples' vanity and argumentative spirit to their immaturity. But others, more mature, also had their disagreements. When Paul and Barnabas, first missionaries of the early church, returned from their first journey together, their friendship erupted into a serious argument before they could begin a second journey.

No Allowance for a Quitter

Paul was ready to embark on the second mission and revisit the towns in Asia Minor where they had preached. He wanted to see how the new believers were doing in the cities of Derbe, Lystra, Iconium, and Antioch.

Barnabas was in agreement, but he wanted to take John Mark with them. The younger man had accompanied them on their first journey but had turned back before they completed their mission and returned to Jerusalem. In chapter 3, we discussed how Mark's expectations may have led to his disappointment and decision to turn back.

Whatever the reason, planning the second journey, "Paul did not think it wise to take him, because he had deserted them in Pamphylia and had not continued with them in the work" (Acts 15:38). Barnabas was not only John Mark's cousin, he was also an encourager. His very name means "son of encouragement." Tenderhearted, forgiving, and wanting to give his relative a second chance, he disagreed with Paul.

The conflict never came to blows, but "they had such a sharp disagreement that they parted company" (Acts 15:39). Barnabas took Mark and sailed for Cyprus (Barnabas's home region), while Paul took Silas and returned to Asia Minor.

We could put a positive spin on it and celebrate the advantages of two missionary parties instead of one. We never hear what happened to Barnabas and Mark because Dr. Luke follows the adventures of Paul through the remainder of Acts. However, we do know that Paul came to value Mark in later years. He wrote to Timothy, "Get Mark and bring him with you, because he is helpful to me in my ministry" (2 Tim. 4:11).

No Tolerance for Hypocrisy

Further conflict erupted in Antioch between Peter and Paul. When Peter came to Antioch, he ate with the Gentiles, something a strict Jew would never do. But Peter was learning to overcome his prejudice and accept his non-Jewish brothers. But when some Jews came from Jerusalem to Antioch, Peter withdrew and separated himself from the Gentiles. Paul said it was "because he was afraid of those who belonged to the circumcision group" (Gal. 2:12).

Not one to allow hypocrisy go unchallenged, Paul confronted "Peter in front of them all [saying], 'You are a Jew, yet you live like a Gentile and not like a Jew. How is it, then, that you force Gentiles to follow Jewish customs?'" (Gal. 2:14).

Even good people, especially strong-willed people, have their differences. Conflict may well be the result. While not excusing conflict, we see it is inevitable. When two live wires touch each other, you will see sparks!

Healthy Church Conflict

Is there such a thing as healthy church conflict? Isn't that an oxymoron, like the term *civil war*? Eric Reed noted that talking about the virtues of conflict reminds us of those commercials about certain medications. After touting the benefits of a new drug, the announcer goes on to give the warnings and disclaimers. In the end, the cure sounds worse than the disease.

Reed imagines that such an ad proclaiming the health benefits of conflict might end with: "Conflict may cause headaches, nausea, and upset stomach. Conflict is not for nursing mothers, those with a history of heart disease, or those on mood-altering drugs. In a few cases, conflict has been known to cause seizures, paralysis, and death."[1]

―――――

Insights on Managing Conflict

Church growth authority Gary L. McIntosh offers four insights regarding three types of conflict, which may be:

1. Interpersonal—conflict with people.
2. Intrapersonal—conflict with ourselves.
3. Substantive—conflict over issues.

Insight 1: Substantive conflict generates interpersonal and intrapersonal conflict. Disagreement on issues may often degenerate into conflict.

Insight 2: Eighty percent of church conflicts are over methods and procedures. Most conflicts arise from differences of opinion on how things are to be done rather than from their underlying values.

Insight 3: People often forget the issue but remember the interpersonal conflict. Personal statements and feelings remain long after the issue is forgotten.

Insight 4: All issues are not equally important. Only rarely are they substantive enough to fight over.

Conflict Is an Opportunity

In reality, conflict is an opportunity. Paul told the Corinthians, "Whether you eat or drink, or whatever you do, do it all for the glory of God. Don't give offense to Jews or Gentiles or the church of God. I, too, try to please everyone in everything I do. I don't just do what is best for me; I do what is best for others so that many may be saved" (1 Cor. 10:31–33 NLT).

In the final analysis, everything we do—even dealing with conflict—must be about what glorifies God and move us closer to the salvation of others. In the heat of debate, being sure our side gets a fair hearing, we may forget this basic principle. It's all about God and reaching others, not simply making our view known or getting our own way.

Conflict Can Be a Control Issue

It is easy for conflict to become a control issue. Even seeking a good thing may ultimately be about who is in control. Someone may say, "I just want to have a godly church," which is a good thing. But who defines what a godly church is? A pastor needs to keep in mind that control issues, even over good things, are often at play.

With that in view, it is helpful to remember James' instruction to us: "What causes fights and quarrels among you? Don't they come from your desires that battle within you? You want something but don't get it. You kill and covet, but you cannot have what you want. You quarrel and fight. You do not have, because you do not ask God. When you ask, you do not receive, because you ask with wrong motives, that you may spend what you get on your pleasures" (James 4:1–3).

+≻= =≺+

Conflicts in a Growing Church

Elmer L. Towns cites seven kinds of conflict in a growing church:

1. Territorial conflicts occur when two or more people want the same responsibility.
2. Border conflicts occur when people do ministry that is perceived to belong to others.
3. Resource conflicts occur when two or more groups within a church use the same resources.
4. Ethnic conflicts arise over racial or ethnic values, but also over traditional and untraditional practices.
5. Influence conflicts may arise when new leaders emerge.
6. Ideological conflicts occur when new people come from different backgrounds.
7. Personality-based conflicts arise between people who don't get along well with one another.

His words may sound harsh, but James had excellent insight. One person says, "I want godly worship, but I want to be sure my style of music predominates." Another says, "I want to reach the lost for Christ, but I don't want it to upset my own preconceived notions of what the church will look like if we have an onslaught of new people." We must keep our focus on Christ and his agenda for the church.

Considering Others' Viewpoints

Closely related to this is the matter of looking at issues from the viewpoint of others. This is a healthy way to deal with conflict. Paul understood this, which is why he challenged the Philippians: "Do nothing out of selfish ambition or vain conceit, but in humility consider others better than yourselves. Each of you should look not only to your own interests, but also to the interests of others" (Phil. 2:3–4).

When we fail to listen to others' viewpoints and insist on having our own way, conflict deepens. But there is a healthier way to deal with the issues. Jim Van Yperen reminds us that there is "a thin line between inviting people into the journey and coercing them." He recommends saying to people, "'We believe God is leading us. I know this is going to be hard for some of you. In fact, some of you won't like it. Will you walk with us as we test God's will here? Will you step out in faith?'—that's leadership. What's *not* leadership is to say, 'Hey, look, this is the way it is. If you don't like it, leave.'"[2]

Covering Up Conflict Is Unhealthy

Covering up the conflict is not a healthy way to proceed. To avoid conflict, we often sweep things under the rug, hope they will go away, minimize the problem, change the subject—you name it. Some of us are very good at avoidance techniques.

But Jesus said, "If your brother sins against you, go and show him his fault, just between the two of you. If he listens to you, you have won your brother over. But if he will not listen, take one or two others along, so that 'every matter may be established by the testimony of two or three witnesses.' If he refuses to listen to them, tell it to the church; and if he refuses to listen even to the church, treat him as you would a pagan or a tax collector" (Matt. 18:15–17).

We need to address conflict sooner rather than later. Waiting usually makes matters worse. Saying we need to address it quickly, however, is not to imply we can resolve it quickly. Conflict resolution requires patience. It requires dependence on the leadership of the Holy Spirit.

Unity Is Not Unanimity

Achieving unity is not the same as unanimity. It is true that Paul said, "Make every effort to keep the unity of the Spirit through the bond of peace" (Eph. 4:3). You will note he did not say we should create unity of the Spirit. Unity exists among people of like faith. It is based on what we have in common through the Lord Jesus Christ. It can fracture and fall apart when people insist on operating unilaterally. But if we can bring people together and encourage them to listen, deferring to one another, even while making their own positions clear, we have a better chance of keeping the unity of the Spirit.

Redeeming Conflict

Adam Clarke, the renowned commentator, said it well: "Nothing is so destructive to the peace of man, and to the peace of the soul, as religious disputes: when they prevail, religion in general has little place."[3] Therefore, every pastor must become a person who improves his or her skill in resolving conflict. Disagreements, even among good people, are inevitable. But they need not get out of hand.

Teach People to Listen to One Another

One of the reasons disagreements escalate into conflict is that we don't listen to one another. Instead of listening, we're often preparing our own arguments to use against the speaker once he or she stops talking. But "listening is such a simple act. It requires us to be present, and that takes practice, but we don't have to do anything else. We don't have to advise, or coach, or sound wise. We just have to be willing to sit there and listen."[4]

People Who Drive People Crazy

Within the church . . . sincere, well-meaning saints . . . leave ulcers, strained relationships, and hard feelings. They don't consider themselves difficult people . . . but they wind up doing more harm than good . . . they drive pastors crazy, or out of the church.

—Marshall Shelley

Have you ever noticed that the last syllable of *listen* is *ten*? It's a good reminder that listening is ten times more effective in avoiding conflict than talking is. If you want the other person's attention, give him or her your attention.

Teach People That Disagreement Is Not Necessarily Negative

Paul and Barnabas disagreed and as a result, two missionary teams went out instead of just one.

However, disagreements do not have to lead to division. Some contrary opinions turn out to be corrective in nature. What husband hasn't been inwardly thankful for his wife's noticing the car coming from the side when he did not see it? He may never want to admit that her scream, unnerving though it was, likely prevented an accident. But her "disagreement" with his driving turned out to be appropriate.

Even if disagreement does not prevent something as dramatic as a collision, rightly understood, a different opinion offers an alternative viewpoint that may be extremely helpful. Our problem is that we are so sure that we are right, we're not ready to listen to another's opinion. The wise pastor welcomes questions and alternative opinions that strengthen the board's understanding of all sides of an issue.

Unresolved Conflict

From 1347 to 1351, the pandemic plague known as the Black Death is estimated to have reduced the world's population from 450 million to between 350 million and 375 million. Unresolved conflict can be equally destructive to God's work. Marriages dissolve, churches split, and Christian organizations implode. But Jesus gave us the cure in Matthew 18:15–17, so administer God's good medicine to protect the health of your team.

—Sue Edwards

C. S. Lewis said, "The Church is not a human society of people united by their natural affinities, but the Body of Christ. . . . All members, however different . . . must share the common life, complementing and helping one another precisely by their differences."[5]

Insist That People Maintain Respect for One Another

I read about a woman who, soon after moving into a small town, complained to her neighbor about the poor service she received at the local drugstore. She hoped the neighbor would pass along her criticism and motivate the druggist to improve.

Imagine her surprise when she visited the drugstore the next time. The druggist greeted her with a big smile, said he was glad to see her, and offered his services to her and her husband in any way he could help. He filled her prescription quickly and efficiently.

The next time she saw her neighbor, she said, "I suppose you told him how poor I thought his service was?"

The neighbor replied, "Well, no, in fact—and I hope you don't mind—I told him you were amazed at the way he had built up this small town drugstore, and that you thought it was one of the best-run drugstores you'd ever seen."[6]

If we all treated each other with respect—even when we are disappointed in someone else's behavior—we would have fewer disagreements. Even when we do disagree, we all appreciate being treated with respect. So let's do the same to others.

Give All Sides a Fair Hearing

There are personalities in every congregation that tend to dominate. Some people always have an opinion on everything and they are not reluctant to let people know what it is. A wise pastor, however, will try to keep things in balance and find ways to give all sides a fair hearing. After hearing from a dominant person, it might be wise to say, "Thank you. I would also like to know some other opinions," and give others a chance to weigh in on the issue in question.

Sometimes it is difficult to hear all sides. Some people just like to fight. They tend to raise their voices, wave their arms, or point fingers. They are in-your-face people. Others simmer in silence. Rather than contribute to the conflict, they remain quiet.

A better approach is when people can calmly express their opinions, examine all sides of the issue, have a civil exchange of ideas, and come to some sort of agreement. This does not mean there will not be tension, but a calm, rational approach is more likely to subdue the tension than the bombastic style of the first group.

Try to Achieve a Consensus

After coalition forces toppled Saddam Hussein and took over the reins of government in Iraq, they soon discovered that conflict was, in many ways, easier than conflict resolution. It was one thing to depose the dictator and quite another to try to put together a democracy.

Even when we calm people down and hear all sides, it may be challenging to achieve a consensus. Yet it is a goal worth pursuing. Everyone can't have everything. Everybody has to give a little. With some common sense and wisdom from the Lord, you can achieve a consensus that will provide a solution pleasing to the Lord and to most of the people.

Remember, even Jesus did not please everyone.

Achieving Consensus

In spite of Cindy's objection, the board decided to move ahead with accepting the district's interest-free loan and complete the project. Fortunately, Cindy cooperated, even though she was initially unhappy with the decision. While a person of strong opinions, she did respect authority. When she saw the rest of the board wanted to move forward, she decided she would not stand in the way.

We can't expect people to act in a way that is contrary to their personalities. Only God can help people see they need to change if a character flaw is involved. But treating people with respect and working to achieve consensus, where that is feasible, can bring clashing personalities together to do what is in the best interest of the church.

Action Steps

1. Make a list of the conflicts you have faced in the church in the past five years. How did you resolve them?
2. What current conflicts may be brewing on the horizon? Are there restless people who may be allowing their unrest to simmer quietly until it boils over? What will you do to head off an explosion?
3. Who are the personalities on your board who tend to clash with one another? List three or four things you might do to bring people together and learn to appreciate each other.

9

TURNOVER
NAVIGATING THE
CHANGING OF THE GUARD

The pastor can influence the next generation of leaders.

Mandy sat in the pastor's office, twisting her handkerchief in her lap while she told him about her busy schedule. Besides teaching school full time and taking care of family responsibilities, she was leading the women's ministry at the church. In addition to those challenges, she was also serving as director of the children's ministry, and she and her husband served as youth sponsors on occasion.

"I just feel pulled in all directions," she said, tears brimming at the corner of her eyes.

Pastor John wondered, in a church of their size, how this one woman had become burdened with all these responsibilities. Having come to the church only a month earlier, he was only beginning to get acquainted with his leaders. In the weeks and months that followed, he would learn that Mandy was a doer—that she tended to take on too many responsibilities. In short, she was a workaholic.

But what he saw immediately in front of him, without the benefit of the insights the succeeding months would bring, was a woman who seemed on the edge of a breakdown.

"It seems like you really have a full plate," he said. "Maybe you should consider dropping something and cutting back on your load a bit."

He paused a moment to gauge her reaction. But seeing only a worried look on her face, he continued, "If you were to drop something, what would it be?"

"I really love the women's ministry," she said, "but I love the children too. Yet if I had to choose, I think I would drop the children's ministry."

"Well, why don't you do that?" Pastor John said.

"I've always felt guilty about giving up a job. Once I accept a responsibility, I really feel I shouldn't let the church down by not giving it my best."

"I appreciate that attitude, Mandy, but one person can only do so much. We'll find someone else to do that job and that should relieve some of your stress."

"I'm relieved that you're not angry with me, Pastor. I know how hard it is to find good workers."

"It's OK, Mandy. I'm giving you permission to lighten your load."

Reasons for Turnover

In the months that followed, Mandy returned to the pastor more than once to thank him for giving her permission to step aside. She was the type of person who felt guilty for not holding up what she perceived to be her share of the load.

Other changes in leadership, including positions on the church board, occur from time to time. Some people, like Mandy, are over-committed and need to be encouraged to do less. Many others are uncommitted and need encouragement to do more. And some others should step aside, but don't for a variety of reasons.

Resignations

Some changes in the board occur because people resign. When a board member resigns in the midst of a term, it needs to be for the right reasons. A person may return from a doctor's visit with less than cheerful news. A health condition may call for a radical change in behavior and schedules. Or the health of a spouse may deteriorate to the point that the other spouse must devote more time to caring for the ill one.

Such resignations are understandable, even if they are regret-table. It is difficult for a pastor to lose a dedicated board member at an inopportune time. The pastor may not have another person ready to step into an experienced board member's shoes on a moment's notice. This is why it's good to have a plan to develop potential board members. We'll address this later.

Anger

When a board member resigns in anger or frustration, a pastor must give the situation special attention. Usually the pastor is aware of conditions that have been brewing to prompt such a sud-den decision. But occasionally, things are simmering behind the scenes and have not been on the pastor's radar. In such cases, he or she must find out as quickly as possible what has precipitated the offended board member's resignation.

Death

Other unexpected changes in the board occur when people die. A pastor received a telephone call one morning from the neighbor of his head usher, who had also been a faithful board member. The usher's five-year-old son had turned up at the neighbor's door early that morning and said he could not wake his father. The boy's mother was away at a conference, so father and son had slept together at the boy's insistence. However, when he woke up and could not rouse his father, he panicked and ran to the neighbor's.

The father had apparently suffered a heart attack in the night. Not only was this a tragic loss to the boy and his mother, it was a sudden loss to the church's leadership team as well.

Other Challenges

Sometimes the composition of the board changes when incumbent board members are not reelected. The pastor must be attentive to those who are unexpectedly terminated. If pastors cannot honestly say, "I'm sorry you were not reelected," they could at least say, "I was surprised when you were not reelected, and I want to thank you for your service to the church. I appreciate your faithfulness to the board through the time of your service."

Others face term limitations, depending on a church's polity, and cannot succeed themselves. Still others choose not to continue in service. They may be tired or discouraged. Again, the pastor must be attentive to these situations and offer pastoral care and counseling when needed, even while considering how to replace the individual who is not continuing in service.

For all these reasons, a pastor may face a changing of the guard. If no thought has been given to prospective board members, and cultivating younger, inexperienced people, a pastor may have the challenge of training new board members "on the job."

Choosing New Leaders

The early apostles faced the sudden loss of their leader when Jesus suffered crucifixion, rose again, then ascended back to heaven. They also faced the loss of one of their own number since Judas Iscariot, despondent after betraying Jesus, hanged himself. One of the first things the apostles did after returning from the Mount of Olives after Jesus' ascension was to meet in the upper room.

Experience

Experience is a hard teacher because she gives the test first, the lesson afterwards.
—Vernon Sanders Law

They were all there—all but Judas Iscariot. Joining them, not only in the room, but also in prayer, were some of the women, Mary the mother of Jesus, and Jesus' brothers.

Peter took the leadership. He stood before the group, which numbered about 120, and said, "Brothers, the Scripture had to be fulfilled which the Holy Spirit spoke long ago through the mouth of David concerning Judas, who served as guide for those who arrested Jesus—he was one of our number and shared in this ministry" (Acts 1:16–17).

A Plan for Replacing Leaders

Quoting from Psalm 109:8, Peter said, "May another take his place of leadership" (Acts 1:20). Based on this understanding of the ancient text, Peter proposed that the group choose another to take Judas's place. He said it should be someone who had been with them the whole time, from the days of John's baptism at the Jordan until the death of Jesus, and a witness of the resurrection.

So two men's names were proposed: Joseph called Barsabbas (also known as Justus) and Matthias. "Then they prayed, 'Lord, you know everyone's heart. Show us which of these two you have chosen to take over this apostolic ministry, which Judas left to go where he belongs'" (Acts 1:24–25).

After praying, they cast lots; the lot fell to Matthias. So by this method, they chose Judas's replacement.

The Right Leader

Some have suggested that this was the wrong selection method, and that eventually the apostle Paul would have filled the vacancy. Though Matthias is never mentioned again, that alone does not mean his election was a mistake. If we consider the criteria Peter and the others used in choosing Matthias, it might be instructive for us.

First, Peter quoted two Old Testament psalms (69 and 109) and applied these references to Judas's situation. We have no record that the others in the upper room disputed with Peter about applying these sacred texts to Judas. Neither did Luke, who wrote the account, criticize the method.

Then, Peter defined the criteria for the open position. The candidates should be those who walked with Jesus from the beginning, and they should be those who witnessed the resurrection. They proposed the names of Joseph and Matthias, but why only those two? Perhaps there were not many who could claim to meet these criteria.

Finally, they prayed, asking the Lord to guide their decision, resulting in Matthias's election. These three methods: Scripture, common sense (defining the criteria), and prayer "constitute a wholesome combination through which God may be trusted to guide us today."[1] Most churches no longer cast lots, but we do cast ballots, and elect many of our board members with just such a procedure.

Conferred Leadership

Centuries earlier, another transition occurred. Elijah had been Elisha's mentor, but the time came when the older man was about to leave.

> Elijah said to Elisha, "Tell me, what can I do for you before I am taken from you?" "Let me inherit a double portion of your spirit," Elisha replied. "You have asked a difficult thing," Elijah said, "yet if you see me when I am taken from you, it will be yours—otherwise not." As they were walking along and talking together, suddenly a chariot of fire and horses of fire appeared and separated the two of them, and Elijah went up to heaven in a whirlwind. . . . [Elisha] picked up the cloak that had fallen from Elijah and went back and stood on the bank of the Jordan. Then he took the cloak that had fallen from him and struck the water with it. . . . When he struck the water, it divided to the right and to the left, and he crossed over. (2 Kings 2:9–11, 13–14)

In the King James Version, *cloak* is translated *mantle*. Since that time, the word *mantle* has come to mean not only a loose, sleeveless cloak, but also a figurative symbol of authority or responsibility.[2] When someone's mantle falls on another, it is a symbol of authority and responsibility being transferred from one to another.

When a board member retires, resigns, or fails to be reelected, that mantle of responsibility falls to the next person who is elected. A wise pastor will capture this concept and endeavor to instill a deep sense of the responsibilities inherent in serving on the church board. By default, board members are seen as spiritual leaders. Others look to them not only for guidance in the business affairs of the church, but to set an example of holy living, to conduct themselves with integrity, and to set a godly pace for others.

So with these two biblical examples—one from the New Testament and one from the Old—we have concepts that can guide us in dealing with turnover on the board. The Scripture's qualifications of leaders (see 1 Tim. 3:1–13; Titus 1:6–9), common sense to recommend persons who are qualified, and prayer to seek the mind of the Lord can serve us well in the election process. Then to instill a sense of responsibility as one person or group takes on the mantle of authority and responsibility can help them soberly and righteously move forward.

Communicating Your Heart for Leadership

Change is inevitable. Transition will occur in every church board from time to time. Churches who have had the same treasurer for thirty years may wonder if this is true, especially if the treasurer has been extremely protective of the church's money to the point of hindering progress. But sooner or later, boards change personnel.

To keep from being caught unprepared when changes occur, a wise pastor will formulate a plan to develop prospective board members. What are the advantages of a regular, systematic way of finding and discipling prospective leaders? It gives you the opportunity to pour into their lives important concepts that will prepare them to assume leadership roles.

Your Passion for God

You will communicate your passion for God through your preaching, of course. But in small group settings, as well as one-on-one opportunities, you will share your passion for putting God first in every area of your life.

The Indispensability of Prayer. As your young leaders get to know you, they will discover that you do more than talk about prayer. They will learn that prayer occupies an indispensable part of your life. As they hear you pray for them, experience your prayers with them, and witness your compassionate prayers for others, they will learn that prayer is part of the fiber of a truly godly leader.

Passion

Passion develops when we are doing what we are designed to do.

—John Townsend

The Importance of the Word. Your prospective leaders will also pick up on the truth that God's Word is not just a launching pad for sermons. They will discover that for you, it is "a lamp to [your] feet and a light for [your] path" (Ps. 119:105). Your example will teach them to turn to God's Word for daily guidance because it contains the words of life.

The Necessity of Worship. If you truly enter into worship in music, prayers, and the reading of the Word, as well as putting yourself energetically into your sermon, your example will resonate authenticity.

Your Vision for the Church

As you spend time with your prospective leaders, whether formally teaching or simply living among them, they will learn that you have a vision for the church. As much as you love the people and all the church stands for, you are not content for the church to remain where it is. You envision more for the congregation, not only more people worshiping together, but greater outreach and ministry to the community. A vision "establishes priorities. It attracts people. And vision defines success."[3] All this will become obvious to your prospective leaders as they watch, listen, and interact with you.

Your Integrity as a Person

If your prospective leaders do not see personal integrity practiced in your daily life, you can forget their ever wanting to follow you in the leadership of the church. It is tempting to cut corners, to be less than honest, to think the rules don't apply to us. But they do. Wayne Schmidt, using Shadrach, Meshach, and Abednego as examples of refusing to bow in the face of incredible power, says, "None of us risk being thrown into a fiery furnace when we stand for our convictions. But we may pay a price. . . . When faced with

Integrity

Tom Mullins observes that fifteen hundred people lost their lives in 1912 when the *Titanic* went down. Only six small slits compromised the hull of that great ship. All too often, it's the small things in our own lives that compromise our integrity. Even the smallest missteps can have a terrible impact.

148

such a situation, it will be tempting to cast the unethical or immoral behavior in the most righteous of terms."[4]

Your young leaders are watching. Don't let them down. Be a person of integrity.

Your Skills as a Leader

As you grow in your leadership skills, you will set an example for those who are watching you. They will observe such things as how you use your time; whether you meet deadlines or procrastinate; whether you are a self-starter or someone has to prime your pump; how you take initiative; whether you can sustain your personal motivation; how you make decisions; and how you deal with problems.

Some of your potential leaders are already leaders in their own sphere of business, education, or industry. You may be able to learn from them. But they are still watching, listening, and learning.

Your Example as a Spouse and Parent

How do you treat your spouse? Others are watching. How do you treat your children? Others are observing. All these behaviors are lived out in the fishbowl we call ministry. You can complain about living in a fishbowl if you want to, but the truth is, every pastor and family do. So make the best of it. Get on the same page with your spouse. Set an example of having regular date nights. Work together to be the best parents you can be, realizing that, like every other parent, you will make mistakes. But if you are committed to being a close couple and consistent parents, balancing love and discipline, your example will pay big dividends.

In these five ways—and others—you have the opportunity to influence your prospective board members. When a sudden turnover occurs, you will know you have been pouring yourself into the next generation of leaders.

How to Develop New Leaders

Every vacancy on the board provides you with an opportunity. When a mature, seasoned member of the board dies, moves away, or retires, you may feel the loss very keenly. You look around and there is no one who can fill the shoes. It's true that you cannot replace maturity overnight, unless you happen to have another seasoned member who can step into that position.

But what if you don't? What if you only have younger, inexperienced members? That is not all bad. What your members lack in maturity, they may be able to make up for with new ideas and teachability. If new board members are teachable and open to being discipled, you have almost unlimited possibilities before you.

Teachability

We often think of Jonathan Edwards as a severe preacher who delivered sermons that condemned others to hell, like his classic "Sinners in the Hands of an Angry God." Yet Edwards possessed a teachable spirit. He wrote in his diary on November 22, 1772, a determination "that I will, if I can by any convenient means, learn what faults others find in me, or what things they see in me, that appear anyway blameworthy, unlovely or unbecoming." The first step in teachability is to recognize where we have fallen short.

A New Crop of Leaders

A friend of mine was elected as district superintendent in an area of the country where he had not previously served. He knew almost no one in the district when he took office. They had elected him because of his superior's recommendation and the interviewing process.

Within the first eighteen months of his tenure, nearly half the pastors changed. In some cases, pastors retired. In other cases, they moved out of his district. As a result, he brought in pastors who also did not have experience in that district.

The downside was that they did not know the culture of that district. The upside was that the new pastors were loyal to him because he had influenced them to come or influenced the churches to consider them. Over time, they established a new culture, keeping the best of what was already there, but adding new elements that improved the effectiveness of that district's operation.

A similar thing can happen when a board changes its composition. New board members add fresh ideas, a new perspective, and a new attitude. But how is a pastor to ensure that new board members will be a positive addition and not a negative force? There may be no foolproof method to guarantee a positive outcome. But many churches have used a method of discipling prospective board members that eased the pain of turnover.

A Pastor's Prayer Partner System

My friend John Maxwell taught hundreds of churches across North America to develop a system of prayer partners to support pastors. John contended that prayer is the power that can change the world. John Wesley said, "Give me 100 preachers who fear nothing but sin and desire nothing but God, and I care not a straw whether they be clergy or laymen, such alone will shake the gates of hell and set up the kingdom of Heaven on earth. God does nothing but in answer to prayer."[5]

In a nutshell, the prayer partner system worked well because it expected regular participation in meeting the pastor each Sunday morning before the worship service for a time of prayer. In some cases, some of the prayer partners would continue to pray for the pastor during the service in a separate location in the church.

But the prayer partner system is not a one-way street, in which the pastor derives all the benefit while the laypersons do all the hard work of praying. The pastor conducts regular times of discipling the prayer partners. An annual prayer retreat might kick off a campaign to recruit prayer partners. At this retreat, the pastor literally teaches the people to pray. The content of the teaching may vary from pastor to pastor, but basically it includes such things as:

- How to structure a time of daily devotion
- How to combat the factors of life that work against prayer
- How to pray for others (being an effective intercessor)
- How to support the pastor in prayer
- How to pray for the church
- How to be an effective member of a prayer team

In addition to an annual prayer retreat, the pastor will want to conduct at least quarterly prayer breakfasts that will provide opportunity for fellowship with the prayer partners, further instruction in prayer and leadership principles, and motivation to continue in effective prayer. It is relatively easy to begin a project like this; it is more difficult to keep it going.

Keep It Going

The pastor will want to enlist helpers who can oversee some of the organizational aspects of a prayer partner system. Regular contacts with the prayer partners through e-mails, text messages, and phone calls can keep the plan going. Neglecting to follow up is a sure way to kill the project. Because we are human, even well-intentioned people forget their responsibilities on occasion without reminders.

How does this system help you recruit and develop leaders for your board? As Maxwell says, "You learn a lot about people when you pray with them, especially about their spiritual maturity."[6] As you interact with your prayer partners on a weekly basis, you will learn to spot those who develop a heart for God and the church. When openings occur in your board—or when it is time for the nominating committee to meet to consider persons to serve for the following year—you will want to keep in mind those prayer partners who have shown the most promise.

Prayer

A life of prayer makes us stronger. E. Stanley Jones, at the age of eighty, suffered impaired speech and paralysis of his writing hand because of a stroke that forced him to remain bedridden. Nevertheless, if he wondered whether he could handle some crisis, he would tell himself, "The innermost strands are the strongest. I need no outer props to hold up my faith."

Baseball teams have farm clubs. Churches can develop farm teams too, cultivating people through prayer with and for them. As you invest yourself in people, they will become more willing to invest in your ministry and the ministry of the church.

Be Prepared

Turnover is inevitable. Every pastor faces this challenge. Since we know it is going to happen, why not prepare and turn turnover into an opportunity to improve the quality of church leadership whenever it is possible?

You can do nothing and accept whoever happens to be available and willing at the time an opening occurs. You can appreciate the heart of a willing person, but these people are not always the best qualified or the most adequately prepared to serve in leadership positions.

Instead of just letting life happen, why not take initiative? Develop a plan to disciple prospective leaders. Through prayer, Bible study, and common sense, you can discern God's plan for your church. By conscientiously developing your people, you can build a stable of potential leaders. When the time comes to change, you will be ready—and so will they.

Action Steps

1. Think about the last time a leadership vacancy occurred in your church. How was it filled? Who made the decision as to whom would serve? Did you get the best person for the job?
2. What is happening in your church now to disciple future leaders?
3. As you think about the possibilities in your church, what initiative do you need to take to develop others so that, when leadership vacancies occur, you will have qualified people ready to serve?

10

ORIENTATION
EQUIPPING NEW BOARD MEMBERS

*Effective pastors will prepare board members
for meaningful service.*

Pastor Tom drove away from the church with a heavy heart. Once again, the board had refused to cooperate with his plans.

"I just don't understand it," he thought. "I prepared well for the meeting, tried to give them all the advantages, and balance it with a list of the disadvantages. I thought I made a convincing case, but they just don't seem to get it.

"I wonder if I'm really cut out for ministry. It doesn't seem like it should be this hard. The board just doesn't share my passion for ministry. The members don't seem to understand how church is supposed to work. Otherwise, would why do they resist every forward move I try to take?"

Turning into his driveway and pushing the remote for the garage door, he thought, "It's almost like we're on different teams. And right now the score is Board 12, Pastor 0. It seems like in the past year, I haven't gotten them to budge on any significant issue. Each month it's the same thing."

Tom's wife, Ellen, had already gone to bed by the time he entered the house. The board meeting had been another long one, and she had to get up early for her job as a nurse at the hospital. He quietly got ready for bed and slipped in beside her. He lay awake for a long time before finally dozing off for another fitful night of tossing and turning.

Pitfalls of Training

Although Tom's problems relate to a church with many experienced board members—at least in terms of years of service—the problems also relate to the way board members are trained—or not trained—from the very outset of their service. The fact is that most board members receive no training in how to be leaders in a church. Likely, no one has ever taught them how to think strategically. They may not be decision makers by training or experience.

Although Tom is learning leadership principles and applying them to his own life and responsibilities, he is experiencing what Larry Osborne calls "educational separation" from his board.[1] Every time Tom reads another leadership book or attends another professional seminar, the gap between him and the board widens.

It represents an inevitable problem when a pastor has no program of board orientation or ongoing training process for the governing board. Good people—even spiritual people—often slow or stall the church's progress simply because they have not been prepared to join the pastor in effective leadership. Even if a pastor implements a process of orientation and training for board members, there are certain pitfalls to avoid.

Lobbying or Training?

For instance, Osborne mentions the difference between lobbying and training. When pastors present training in the midst of a decision-making process, it is easy for board members to feel they are being lobbied rather than trained.

A pastor can easily fall into this trap. Pastors get excited about a new program, staff member, or direction. They realize the board may not be up to speed with the new ideas. This is an ideal time to present a teaching session, outlining the advantages, clarifying the finer points, and instilling new concepts that will help the board accept the new idea. Yet we must be careful that we don't come across as trying to "sell" them. Presented at another time, apart from the pending decision, the training session may resonate beautifully with the board members.

Highlighting the Training

I know many pastors who use the first part of their board meeting time as an ideal opportunity to train their board members. It makes sense, on the face of it. They are already there; it does not require an extra meeting; and it is a positive use of the time.

Communication

A simple principle of communication says this: everyone has three buttons on their forehead. If you push the red button, you cause people to stop listening; you turn them off. If you push the yellow button, you cause them to be cautious. If you push the green button, you gain acceptance and agreement; they "go" with you as you teach. Do your best to push only green buttons.

However, it may come across to the board members as preliminary to the real reason they have come—to deal with the business of the church. Consequently, they may listen politely but in fact are tuning out the pastor, while they wait for the important stuff to begin.

By planning a specific time for training—whether it is a monthly meeting, a quarterly retreat, or an occasional event, it becomes a significant stand-alone experience. By giving the training session its own day and time, it increases its importance and heightens its value to the members.

Time to Marinate

Because you already know and understand the concepts you are teaching, it is easy to feel the board should get it with one hearing. This is usually not the case. You may think that repeating an idea you have already taught will bore the board. But people need to hear a new idea more than once before they accept it as their own. Osborne contends for three stages to learning.

Exposure. This is the first time the idea is heard. It may be exciting, a new and fresh approach to the problems with which your church wrestles. But it's only a first exposure.

Familiarity. At this stage, board members have heard it before but not fully bought into it yet. The idea lacks the excitement of newness, and the temptation may be to move on to something else.

Understanding. At the understanding stage, people are not just familiar with the idea, they have also reached the point where they can teach it to others. They know how to apply the concept. They have not fully learned, says Osborne, until they reach this stage.[2]

Even after people have been through the three stages, you may need to continue to repeat some of the concepts from time to time.

Power and Presence

When Jesus began his ministry, all his board members (disciples) were new. How did he equip them to lead? How did he prepare them to serve?

We find the answers, not only in observing what Jesus did with them and how he treated them, but also in what others observed after he was gone. When Jesus ascended to heaven following his resurrection, the disciples returned to Jerusalem, entered an upper room, and waited for the Holy Spirit to come. In fact, just before leaving them, Jesus said, "I am going to send you what my Father has promised; but stay in the city until you have been clothed with power from on high" (Luke 24:49).

The Holy Spirit came and filled them on the day of Pentecost. In the fullness of this new power, Peter and the others began to preach and teach in the name of Jesus. Because they taught that Jesus had risen from the dead, the religious authorities arrested Peter and John and put them in jail. The next day, the rulers brought the apostles before them and demanded to know by whose power or in whose name they taught these things.

Peter answered, "If we are being called to account today for an act of kindness shown to a cripple and are asked how he was healed, then know this, you and all the people of Israel: It is by the name of Jesus Christ of Nazareth, whom you crucified but whom God raised from the dead, that this man stands before you healed" (Acts 4:9–10). He went on to remind them that they had rejected Jesus. Yet he told them, "Salvation is found in no one else, for there is no other name under heaven given to men by which we must be saved" (Acts 4:12).

The observation of the Jewish leaders is revealing: "When they saw the courage of Peter and John and realized that they were unschooled, ordinary men, they were astonished and they took note that these men had been with Jesus" (Acts 4:13).

Their observation shows us three major ways that Jesus had prepared them for leadership.

Fear Turned to Courage

They had become men of courage. Without question, the primary reason they were courageous was that they had been filled with the Holy Spirit. No one would have accused Peter of being courageous after he denied the Lord three times. What could change him from a man who denied the Lord into a man who stood up to the very religious authorities who had succeeded in crucifying Jesus?

Only the power of the Holy Spirit could accomplish such a remarkable transformation. Between the two experiences, Peter experienced Pentecost.

Courage

No captain can do very wrong if he places his ship alongside that of the enemy. . . . All problems, personal, national, or combat, become smaller if you don't dodge them. Touch a thistle timidly and it pricks you; grasp it boldly and its spines crumble. Carry the battle to the enemy. Lay your ship alongside his.

—Admiral Lord Nelson

Ordinary Turned Extraordinary

They were unschooled, ordinary men. In other words, their boldness had nothing to do with their being seminary trained or theologically educated. They were fishermen, tax collectors, ordinary people who pursued ordinary lives prior to spending time with Jesus. Obviously, their three-plus years with him were valuable beyond measure. But they were not the products of formal training as it was known and understood in that era.

So whatever training we provide to our board members today, as important as it may be, should not be offered to the exclusion of time spent in personal encounter with the pastor. While we should never eliminate structured training, we also must observe that more is caught than taught. Mentoring, whether from the pastor or peers, is equally as valuable as formal instruction.

The Power of Presence

The authorities observed that Peter and John "had been with Jesus" (Acts 4:13). Was this simply a recognition of the fact that they had been his disciples in the same way other Jewish rabbis had groups of disciples who spent time with them? Perhaps, but it was more than that. No one could spend time in the presence of Jesus without being profoundly influenced by him.

Even Judas was deeply affected by his time spent with Jesus. He seemed to have had no malicious intent in betraying Jesus, because he felt deep regret upon realizing the enormous consequences of his betrayal for thirty pieces of silver. Matthew told us that Judas was "seized with remorse" when he saw that Jesus was condemned to death. Judas "returned the thirty silver coins to the chief priests and the elders. 'I have sinned,' he said, 'for I have betrayed innocent blood'" (Matt. 27:3–4).

Mentoring Relationships

Paul understood the importance of spending time with his protégés. Timothy, Titus, Silas, Luke, and others benefited from their travels and adventures with the apostle. In Romans 16, Paul compiled a long list of associates for whom he was grateful. They all profited from their contact with Paul.

Priscilla and Aquila spent many hours with him. Their loyalty was unmatched. Paul was a dangerous man to be around and "they risked their lives" for the apostle (Rom. 16:4).

Andronicus and Junias spent time in prison with Paul (Rom. 16:7). He did not tell us where, when, or for how long, but he said they were "outstanding among the apostles." We can be sure that if they spent time with Paul, he mentored them. They may have enjoyed some mutual mentoring since "they were in Christ before [Paul] was."

Rufus was another close friend of Paul's. They must have spent many hours together because Rufus's mother was like a mother to Paul (Rom. 16:13). Precisely what that means we do not know. But it does mean that Rufus and his mother spent enough time with Paul that there must have been a mentoring relationship.

Mentoring

Leighton Ford, speaking about his focus on developing leaders in their late twenties and thirties, said: "We work to sharpen their vision, shape their values, and share their ventures."

Spending time with either Jesus or Paul produced people of courage, loyalty, and commitment. The same holds true of disciples today. Paul laid down this principle of discipleship when he told Timothy, "And the things you have heard me say in the presence of many witnesses entrust to reliable men who will also be qualified to teach others" (2 Tim. 2:2).

Equipping Leaders

One of the most important things to teach new leaders—as well as older leaders who have not yet learned it—is how to lead. Most lay leaders have never had any formal training in leadership. They may think they are leaders simply because they have been elected to a position of leadership. While there is a degree of truth to that idea, it does not begin to encompass the meaning of leadership.

The Meaning of Leadership

Leadership has been defined as "to think long-range, to motivate followers, to solve problems."[3]

To think long-range is a valuable skill. Many people never think any further ahead than their next paycheck or next summer's vacation. Leading the board in assessing where you are and where you need to go is vitally important. If a new board member has never engaged in such a process, he or she will, if wise, listen and learn from others.

Encouraging board members to be visionary will assist them in long-range planning. Help them think not just about how things are, but how they could be. Dream about possibilities. Then define some clear objectives to be accomplished and determine some responsibilities for who will accomplish what. These are all important steps in long-range planning to which new board members will become exposed.

Motivating followers is another skill that is important for board members to learn. This is the point at which the pastor can help board members realize that leadership derives from their influence, not their position. As members of the leadership team, they will have influence with others in the church. As church members support the board's direction with enthusiasm, this will influence and motivate others in the church to get on board.

Solving problems is a third skill needed by every board member. One of the best things a pastor can instill in his or her board members is a positive attitude that believes problems can be solved. Find a way early in your tenure to combat the idea that "We've never done it that way before" or "We tried that before, and it didn't work." That kind of negativity will throw cold water on the best of plans.

Bill Bright was a great example of a problem solver who viewed life with a "can-do" attitude. After his death, Bright's son Brad told about a reporter from a Christian magazine who asked his father, "Dr. Bright, share with us an example from your own life about a problem you face that the average Joe Christian can relate to."

Bright said, "I don't have any problems."

The reporter said, "Don't overspiritualize this, we all have problems." The reporter pressed on, asking the question several different ways.

Finally Bright said, "Young man, you need to understand that *I understand* that I am a slave of Jesus, and a slave doesn't have problems. The only thing the slave has to do is what the master asks of him. He doesn't have to be successful, and when you really understand that, all of a sudden you don't have problems anymore. All that's left is opportunities to see God work."[4]

If you can internalize that concept so that you believe it and can communicate it to your board members, you will have accomplished a vital step in the orientation and equipping process. You will have helped them see that problems are opportunities in disguise. When you believe that, "nothing will be impossible for you" (Matt. 17:20).

Expectations

Besides teaching the board members to understand what leadership is, you must help them know the expectations. Much of this may be accomplished even in the recruiting stage of preparing them for board membership. In other words, before you secure their agreement to let them run for election to a board position, they have a right to know what is expected of them.

For instance, what is the term of service? In most cases, it will be for a year, although some positions may be for terms of two or three years.

How many meetings will they need to attend, and how often? Will they meet monthly? Quarterly?

What kind of time commitment will they be expected to give? Will there be typically one three-hour meeting monthly, or will there be an expectation to spend other days, nights, or hours in some obligation as a member of the board?

In addition to the time commitments, new members need to know if additional committee assignments are part of the expectations. Obviously, a treasurer would expect to serve on a finance committee. A trustee would expect to meet at other times to consider building and property concerns. What about the other board members?

How Things Work

How do things work in this church? Do you operate by strict parliamentary procedures, using *Robert's Rules of Order*? Or are the meetings more casual? Do most actions of the board rise out of committee work, which is then presented to the board as formal resolutions, or are members free to propose ideas spontaneously? Some idea of how things work will be helpful in orienting new board members.

On-the-Job Training

It is impossible to cover everything in an initial orientation. So at least some on-the-job training is necessary. We learn as we go. Hopefully, it will not be as painful or as anxious as the rookie soldier in the *Hagar the Horrible* cartoon. In the midst of the battle, with a horde of enemies approaching from all sides, Hagar says to the rookie, "No, no! Hold your shield higher and swing your sword like this!" To which the rookie, looking at the reader, says, "I hate 'on the job training'!!"[5]

Equipping board members is one of the most important things a pastor does. Sue Mallory believes a vital aspect of the training is how we invite them to join us in leadership. "Are we inviting them in a way that honors them? Is it a personal invitation that validates their gifts, hearts, and passions?"[6] If so, we're off to a good start.

What They Need to Know

Besides the nuts and bolts of how the board is organized, how the church works, the meaning of leadership, and the basic expectations, what are the most important things your new board members need to know?

Let Them See Your Heart

What are you passionate about? What makes your heart beat faster, increases your adrenalin, and causes you to stay up late and get up early?

At the Methodist Center, Epworth-by-the-Sea at St. Simon's Island, Georgia, is a marker placed there by Bishop Arthur Moore. It bears this inscription: "Let us read the story of John Wesley again. This cultured, conscientious gentleman, resolute in self-denial, punctual in all observances, doing all the good he could, and avoiding evil, had everything but peace in his own heart. Then the room in Aldersgate Street and his face-to-face confrontation with his Saviour. Presently that masterful little man climbed on his horse to set out on the conquest of England, with only one resource, the assurance given him that Christ had taken away his sins. Soon that spark of grace set ten thousand hearts on fire."[7]

Heart

The heart of a leader is the heartbeat of a group.

—Doug Firebaugh

One of the reasons Wesley accomplished all he did was that his followers could see his heart set ablaze by his love for Christ. As we allow our own hearts to be filled and cleansed by the Spirit, we too can influence others to seek the very best for the church. Let your board members see your heart for God and the church.

Instill a Love for the Church

It has become in vogue in recent years to criticize and minimize the importance of the institutional church. Yet the church is here to stay. As Janie Cheaney observed, "God ordained three institutions: the family, the state, and the church. . . . Of all God-ordained institutions, the church is often the one overlooked—and yet, interestingly, the only one that will last."[8]

She is right. The church is an enduring institution. Somewhere, there used to be a sign that read, "When the building burns down and the preacher leaves town, what you really have left is the church." That's because the church is not about the building. And the church has survived a variety of pastoral leaders, good and bad.

The church is the grand hope for the world. How has God determined to bring the world to himself? Through his followers, who are called the church. "Go and make disciples of all nations," he said (Matt. 28:19). If we don't do it, there is no other plan. No one else will pick up the torch and carry the interests of the kingdom forward. It's up to the church. So we believe in it and we love the church. Instill a love for the church in your board members.

Teach Them to Think Positively

Anyone can criticize. Anyone can be a cup-half-empty person. Anyone can give up before the problem is solved. It takes a person who thinks positively to find solutions and bring those solutions to bear on the thorny issues that boards face.

A pastor-friend told me that when he is looking for a candidate for church treasurer, he looks for a person who thinks positively. If he only looks for someone with accounting skills, he may or may not be able to teach that person positive thinking. If the candidate is reasonably intelligent and has any aptitude for numbers, my friend feels he can teach accounting and bookkeeping skills the applicant needs. But if he begins with a positive thinker, he is miles down the road.

Positive thinkers recognize the opportunities, and they desire to seize them. Positive thinkers help you think through problems instead of being stymied by them. Positive thinkers provide encouragement instead of discouragement. Set an example by your own positive thinking, planning, and presenting.

Teach Them to Think Big

I heard about one young man who thought big. He wrote on his application for a lumberjack's job that he learned his trade in the Sahara Forest. The interviewer said, with a smile, "You mean the Sahara Desert." The young fellow stuck out his chest and said, "Sure, now it is!"

Norman Vincent Peale said, "When you affirm big, believe big, and pray big, big things happen."[9] Thinking big does not necessarily mean you strive for a million-dollar campus for your church or aim for one thousand in worship attendance if you're currently running less than one hundred. What it does mean is that you don't want to be stifled by small-minded thinking.

A big thinker is one who tends to look up and not down. I read about a man who, as a child, found some loose change on the ground. For the rest of his life, he kept looking for money. Forty years later, he had acquired 2,713 pennies, 358 nickels, 210 dimes, six quarters, nine fifty-cent pieces, two silver dollars, and a bent back.[10]

Humility

Citing the need to be humble, even while we think positively, David G. Myers and Malcolm A. Jeeves cite C. S. Lewis's statement: "If anyone would like to acquire humility, I can, I think, tell him the first step. The first step is to realize that one is proud. . . . He and you are two things of such a kind that if you really get into any kind of touch with him you will, in fact, be humble, feeling the infinite relief of having for once got rid of [the pretensions that have] made you restless and unhappy all your life." Myers and Jeeves add, "To be self-affirming yet self-forgetful, positive yet realistic, grace-filled and unpretentious—that is the Christian vision of abundant life."

A small-minded thinker tends to see a problem behind every possibility, an obstacle behind every opportunity, and a crisis behind every challenge. Big thinkers see solutions, answers, and potential for good. Be a big thinker yourself, and teach your board members to think big.

Teach Them to Think Long Term

The easy solutions are the ones that work right now. You and your board will often face the temptation to apply a short-term solution to a long-term problem. You will be tempted to put a Band-Aid on something that requires major surgery. Short-term solutions not only work faster, but they generally cost less, almost always an attractive option.

What you and your board will want to do is envision the right thing for the long run. Sometimes, as one step toward a long-term solution, you can apply a short-term application. You may not be able to add a new educational wing because you need time to develop a sound plan and raise funds. Meanwhile, you may be able to remodel the educational space you have so that you can use the space more efficiently.

You may be tempted to give up on the dream of a new wing altogether because the remodel makes everyone feel good and gives you a little breathing space. However, it does not solve the long-range problem of accommodating the growth you are having or anticipate to have. Don't allow short-term thinking to rob you of blessings that require long-term thinking, planning, and funding.

You can teach many things to your board. But be sure you teach them these basics that will equip them to be better board members, more positive thinkers, and more efficient planners.

A Time for Training

In God's providence, when Pastor Tom rose the next morning after the discouraging board meeting, he picked up a professional journal that included a helpful article on training the church board. As he read the article, he realized there was a gap between his own understanding of how the church works and his board's understanding. He began to think that perhaps their reluctance to follow him was not so much digging in their heels as it was a gap in their thinking.

At the next board meeting, he announced a time on a Saturday morning to meet with the board simply for the purpose of exploring ideas about the church, how things work, and concepts of leadership. Things did not change overnight, but in a few months, he realized the board members were more cooperative than they had ever been before. Over time, they learned to think together, work together, and lead the church forward in positive ways.

Action Steps

1. Compare your own understanding of leadership with your board's understanding. How have they shown their understanding? What attitudes or decisions have they made that would indicate a need for training?

2. What kinds of things have you done to equip your board to be better leaders in the church?

3. If you have not already done so, set a time to equip and train the board. As far as content is concerned, utilize notes from leadership seminars you have attended.

APPENDIX

Chapter 1

Purpose: Understanding the Value of Church Boards

How does one measure the value of a church board? For that matter, how does one measure anything?

Consider these areas of determining value.

Financial Value

What is a church board worth financially? Not the combined total of their net worth, but what are they worth to the church? Naturally, their value cannot be determined solely by finances, but some pastors make it clear to prospective board members that they are expected to set an example for the congregation by tithing their income. While no one but the treasurer or financial secretary may actually know the amount people give, pastors ask board members to be on their honor, either to tithe or resign. A tithing board is of inestimable value to the church because of the power of their example.

Relational Value

What is a church board worth relationally? A supportive board helps to build positive relationships with the rest of the congregation.

This can be of inestimable value when trying to raise support for a capital stewardship campaign or enlisting congregational support for a new direction in which the pastor wants to lead the church. Someone suggested that every board member carries two buckets—a bucket of water and a bucket of gasoline. They can either extinguish a fire or cause it to spread. Positive relationships are extremely valuable.

Vocational Value

A church board with a good work ethic will expect its staff to work hard and be worth the investment the church makes in them. Rightfully so. Church board members with vocational skills can bring added benefit to the church by using those skills to benefit the church. Board members with financial skills may serve on the finance committee. Those with carpentry skills or plumbing skills may serve on the board of trustees. Those with leadership skills in their secular employment can also be gainfully employed as volunteer leaders of the church's various programs and ministries. A board's vocational value is considerable.

Spiritual Value

Board members who are spiritually mature add considerably to the value of the church. Because they believe in prayer, they are supportive of the pastor, staff, and church's ministries. Because they believe in Bible study, they serve as good examples and may even be skilled Bible teachers. Because they believe in the value of truth, they bring integrity to the board meetings as well as sound, spiritually minded judgment. Immature board members can reduce a church's value because they can easily take sides in church squabbles instead of being mature mediators to work with the pastor in guiding the church through the troubles. The spiritual value of board members is high on the list.

Chapter 6
Initiative: Developing Long-Term Strategies[1]

Helping People See a Bigger Picture and Achieve a Better Reality in Christ

What Kind of Church/Ministry Do We Want to Become? (Vision)

- After listing descriptive terms, identify the three priority issues.
- What is our current reality?
- What will be our plan for communicating the vision?
- How can we best get the people to "own" it?

How Do We Get There? (Strategy)

- What does that kind of church actually do?
- Take inventory of resources (human, facility, and financial).
- What organization, mobilization, and delegation will it take?
- Set long-, medium-, and short-range goals to achieve the vision.
- Are the right people doing the right things to achieve the vision?

How Will We Know if We Are Arriving? (Follow-Through)

- This is about assessment, accountability, and adjustment.
- What will be our means of reporting?
- Design measurable, reachable goals.
- Would a timeline chart be useful?
- How can we measure our progress, and where is this discussed?
- What needs to be changed to make progress more likely (mid-course corrections)?

Chapter 8
Conflict: Managing Clashing Opinions and Personalities[2]

If handled correctly, conflict can strengthen the church and give people a reason to believe they can be heard. Improperly handled, conflict may put a major dent in the growth of the church. Here is a checklist for those involved in church conflict:

1. Do you talk to everyone but the person or persons who have the power to change the situation? If you do, you are part of the problem and not the solution.

2. Are you telling neighbors and those from other churches? This will not correct the issue. It only makes your church less attractive to outsiders.

3. Do you find a desire to be in control if you are really honest about your inner feelings? What are your motivations for the position you have taken? Are you genuinely concerned or intent on getting your own way?

4. Do you feel a need to discredit the people who hold an opposing view? To cast aspersions on the credibility of others may happen in courts of law, but it does not belong in the church.

5. Do you slant your story line to make those who disagree with your position seem less Christian than you? Beware of throwing a spiritual cloak of righteousness around your view to the detriment of others.

6. Do you find yourself putting your perceived opponent's character on the line? Do you question his or her motivation,

intent, lifestyle, etc., in order to make his or her position less valid?

7. Do you have a hidden agenda of removing your opponent from the church? Are you shifting from the real problem to a hidden motivation of getting the individual to leave?

8. Do you find yourself counting the people on your "side"?

9. Are you trying to take over leadership that God has placed on another? Taking over may cause you to win temporarily, but God cannot honor your motive.

10. Are you allowing things to die once action has been taken by those in authority? Or do you push until your position is embraced?

Chapter 10
Orientation: Equipping New Board Members[3]

Sample Board Member Orientation Outline

Meeting Format

The goal in orientation is to make the new members feel like an integral part of the board as quickly as possible. Information helps everyone feel at ease. Conduct an orientation session for all new board members as soon as possible. By going over background material about the church, you bring them up to date on the issues facing the board. A question-and-answer time is helpful. Try to cover these topics in a new board member briefing:

Introduce Everyone
- Elected chair
- Executive officers
- Committee chairs and members
- Other board members
- Staff
- Guests and others

Describe the Church (Mission)
- Whom we serve
- What we do
- Overview of programs
- Other

Explain and Discuss

- Meeting attendance requirements—both full board and committee
- Committee assignments and charges
- Board role and relation to administrator or staff
- Conduct facilities tour
- Administrative offices and board room
- Other

Provide Documents Organized in a Manual

- Mission statement
- Policy manual, if any
- Minutes of board meetings for the past year
- Annual report
- Audit report
- Current budget
- Current financial report
- Strategic plan
- Goals for the year
- Roster of board members, including contact information
- List of board officers
- List of committee members, including chairs
- Annual calendar of activities and meetings
- Copies of the newsletter for the year
- Other

Collect Data at the Meeting

- Addresses
- Telephone—home and office

- Fax number
- E-mail address
- Best time to contact
- Best time for meetings
- Other

By conducting an orientation meeting as soon as possible (within the first month of the term of office), you enable new board members to feel comfortable with their responsibilities. You also increase the likelihood of their developing a good working relationship with current members.

NOTES

Chapter 1

1. Peter F. Drucker, *Managing the Non-Profit Organization: Practices and Principles* (New York: HarperCollins, 1990), 178.
2. Cited in Drucker, *Managing the Non-Profit*, 172.
3. H. B. London, Jr., "About Board Meetings," *The Pastor's Weekly Briefing*, Focus on the Family, October 22, 1999, 1.

Chapter 2

1. Stuart Briscoe, *Purifying the Church: What God Expects of You and Your Church* (Ventura, Calif.: Regal, 1987), 43.
2. Ibid.
3. "Harry S. Truman Quotes," BrainyQuote.com, accessed August 30, 2011, http://www.brainyquote.com/quotes/authors/h/harry_s_truman_2.html.
4. Briscoe, *Purifying the Church*, 53–56.
5. Cited in Peter F. Drucker, *Managing the Non-Profit Organization: Practices and Principles* (New York: HarperCollins, 1990), 173.
6. Ibid.
7. Cited in Tricia Rife, "Female Pastor Born to Lead," *Wesleyan Life*, August 31, 2012, http://www.wesleyanlifeonline.com/article/527 (site discontinued).
8. Jim Rohn, "The Four Emotions That Can Lead to Life Change," The-Emotions.com, accessed February 3, 2012, http://www.the-emotions.com/the-four-emotions-life-change.html.

Chapter 3

1. Thinkexist.com, accessed February 7, 2012, http://thinkexist.com/quotation/problems_are_only_opportunities_in_work_clothes/208047.html.

2. "Peter Marshall Quotes," BrainyQuote.com, accessed February 7, 2012, http://www.brainyquote.com/quotes/authors/p/peter_marshall.html.

3. Charles W. Carter and Ralph Earle, *The Acts of the Apostles*, The Evangelical Commentary (Grand Rapids, Mich.: Zondervan, 1959), 181.

4. Cited on Jo Anne Lyon's Facebook page, "Expectations of a Local Board," January 4, 2012, http://www.facebook.com/#!/note.php?note_id=10150563526186458.

Chapter 4

1. Richard K. Wallarab, "A Meeting of the Board" (a satire), *Christianity Today*, January 17, 1979.

2. The Quotations Page, accessed February 21, 2012, http://www.quotationspage.com/quote/1294.html.

3. Stan Toler, "Keys to a Successful Board Meeting," in *Stan Toler's Practical Guide to Pastoral Ministry* (Indianapolis, Ind.: Wesleyan Publishing House, 2007), 294–297.

4. "Planning," Jim Rohn International, accessed February 26, 2012, http://finsecurity.com/homepage/quotes/qm085.html.

5. "Benjamin Disraeli Quotes," BrainyQuote.com, accessed February 26, 2012, http://www.brainyquote.com/quotes/quotes/b/benjamindi130016.html.

6. Quotations Book, accessed February 27, 2012, http://quotationsbook.com/quote/21266.

Chapter 5

1. Adapted from Ron McClung, "Positive Perspective," *Owosso Argus-Press*, May 21, 2011.

2. Peter F. Drucker, *Managing the Non-Profit Organization: Practices and Principles* (New York: HarperCollins, 1990), 140.

3. Alan Nelson, "Vision," *Rev!*, January/February 2006, 49.

4. "Paul J. Meyer Quotes," BrainyQuotes.com, accessed March 7, 2012, http://www.brainyquote.com/quotes/authors/p/paul_j_meyer.html.

Chapter 6

1. J. Oswald Sanders, *Spiritual Leadership* (Chicago: Moody Press, 1980), 156.

2. Dictionary Quotes, accessed April 3, 2012, http://www.dictionary-quotes.com/procrastination-is-opportunity-s-natural-assassin-victor-kiam.

3. "Taking Matters into His Own Hand," *World*, January 26/February 2, 2008, 17.

4. Daily Inspiration—Daily Quote, accessed April 3, 2012, http://www.quotes-daily.com/2009/10/george-washington-carver-quotes-ninety.html.

5. Eugene Cernan and Don Davis, *The Last Man on the Moon* (New York: St. Martin's Press, 1999), 48.

6. Andrew Chaikin, *A Man on the Moon: The Voyages of the Apollo Astronauts* (New York: Viking, 1994), 2.

7. Charles R. Swindoll, *Active Spirituality: A Non-Devotional Guide* (Dallas: Word, 1994), 86.

8. "Quotes on Initiative," Quotation Collection, accessed April 4, 2012, http://www.quotationcollection.com/tag/initiative/quotes.

9. "Thoughts on the Business of Life," Forbes.com, accessed April 4, 2012, http://thoughts.forbes.com/thoughts/beginning-charles-m-schwab-the-difference-between.

10. Andy Stanley, *Visioneering* (Sisters, Ore.: Multnomah, 1999), 31.

11. "Quotations—General," *James S. Huggins' Refrigerator Door* (blog), accessed April 9, 2012, http://www.jamesshuggins.com/h/quo1/quotations_general.htm.

12. Gary L. McIntosh, *Biblical Church Growth: How You Can Work with God to Build a Faithful Church* (Grand Rapids, Mich.: Baker, 2003), 112.

13. Bobb Biehl, *Dream Energy: Make a More Significant Difference . . . By Fulfilling Your Life Dream* (n.p.: Quick Wisdom, 2001), 179.

Chapter 7

1. David L. McKenna, *Mark*, The Communicator's Commentary Series, ed. Lloyd J. Ogilvie (Waco, Tex.: Word, 1982), 139.

2. Stephen C. Tweed, "How to Plan, Organize, and Conduct Your Next Board/Staff Retreat," accessed April 11, 2012, http://www.leadinghomecare.com/docs/Board%20Retreat%20Article%20PDF.pdf.

3. Ibid., 2.

4. "On Concentration/Focus," Jim Rohn International, accessed April 16, 2012, http://vsa.fsonline.com/quotes/qm0065.html.

5. Tom Phillips, "Building a Team to Get the Job Done," in *Leaders on Leadership: Wisdom, Advice and Encouragement on the Art of Leading God's People*, ed. George Barna (Ventura, Calif.: Regal, 1997), 222.

6. Colleen Francis, "Being Honest with Yourself," Ideal Marketers, accessed April 16, 2012, http://www.ideamarketers.com/?Being_Honest_With_Yourself&articleid=658005 (site discontinued).

7. This section was more fully developed in a chapter of my book, "Directing Attention," in *Stan Toler's Practical Guide for Pastoral Ministry* (Indianapolis, Ind.: Wesleyan Publishing House, 2007), 184–186.

8. "Storyboard," Wikipedia, accessed April 17, 2012, http://en.wikipedia.org/wiki/Storyboard.

Chapter 8

1. Cited by Marshall Shelley, "Resolutely Redemptive," *Leadership*, Fall 2004, 3.

2. Jim Van Yperen, "Keeping Conflict Healthy: The Leadership Forum," *Leadership*, Fall 2004, 24.

3. Cited by Earle L. Wilson, Alex R. G. Deasley, and Barry L. Callen, *Galatians, Philippians, Colossians*, A Commentary for Bible Students (Indianapolis, Ind.: Wesleyan Publishing House, 2007), 118.

4. Cited by Mark O. Wilson, "Love Is in the Listening," *Wesleyan Life*, Summer 2011, 13.

5. Cited by Charles Colson, "Squabbling Christian Soldiers: Disunity in the Body," *Breakpoint* radio commentary, May 15, 2003.

6. John C. Maxwell and Jim Dornan, *Becoming a Person of Influence*, (Nashville: Thomas Nelson, 1997), 42.

Chapter 9

1. John Stott, *The Spirit, the Church, and the World: The Message of Acts* (Downers Grove, Ill.: InterVarsity Press, 1990), 59.

2. "Mantle," Your Dictionary, accessed May 8, 2012, http://www.yourdictionary.com/mantle.

3. Jim Dethmer, "Becoming a Visionary Leader through Clear Personal Vision," *Ministry Advantage*, July/August 1994, 1.

4. Wayne Schmidt, "Personal Integrity," *Wesleyan Life*, Fall 2006, 4.
5. Cited by John Maxwell, *Partners in Prayer* (Nashville: Thomas Nelson, 1996), 7.
6. Ibid., 111.

Chapter 10

1. Larry Osborne, "Why Board Training Goes Awry," *Leadership Journal*, Summer 1987, 120.
2. Ibid., 122–123.
3. Ibid., 123.
4. "Bill Bright's Legacy: A Rev! Interview with Brad Bright," *Rev!*, July/August 2007, 34.
5. King Features Syndicate, reprinted by John C. Maxwell, *Developing the Leaders Around You* (Nashville: Thomas Nelson, 1995), 99.
6. "The Art of Equipping: An Interview with Sue Malloy," *Rev!*, January/February 2006, 90.
7. Attributed to Vance Havner, *Song at Twilight*, cited in *New Beginnings*, newsletter (Waterloo, Iowa: First Wesleyan Church, June 2002), 2.
8. Janie B. Cheaney, "Truly Exceptional," *World*, April 24, 2010, 26.
9. "President's Society," Johnston Community College Foundation, accessed May 20, 2012, http://www.johnstoncc.edu/foundation/major donorscumulative.aspx.
10. Norman Vincent Peale and Donald T. Kauffman, *Bible Power for Successful Living: Helping You Solve Everyday Problems* (Pawling, N.Y.: Peale Center for Christian Living, 1993), 180.

Appendix

1. Adapted from a seminar by David Holdren, under the auspices of the Leadership Development Journey of The Wesleyan Church.
2. Adapted from Ronald Kelly, "A Church Conflict Checklist," *The Wesleyan Advocate*, February 1995, 24.
3. Adapted from the United Way of Minneapolis Area, "Create the Future," accessed May 18, 2012, http://www.createthefuture.com/board_orientation_tools.htm.

Real Help for Real Pastors!

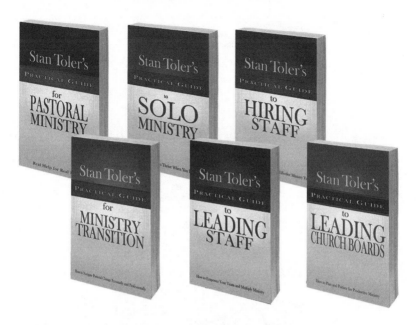

Whether you are new to ministry of have been in ministry for several years, Stan Toler can help as you face the difficult situations that come with leading churches and people. Based on years of pastoral and leadership experience with all sizes and types of churches and organizations, Stan provides practical answers on over a hundred topics and offers an abundance of encouragement and affirmation.

Titles in this series include—

Stan Toler's Practical Guide for
Pastoral Ministry
ISBN: 978-0-89827-612-1

Stan Toler's Practical Guide to
Solo Ministry
ISBN: 978-0-89827-383-0

Stan Toler's Practical Guide to
Hiring Staff
ISBN: 978-0-89827-384-7

Stan Toler's Practical Guide to
Ministry Transition
ISBN: 978-0-89827-385-4

Stan Toler's Practical Guide to
Leading Staff
ISBN: 978-0-89827-597-1

Stan Toler's Practical Guide to
Leading Church Boards
ISBN: 978-0-89827-596-4

wesleyan
publishing
house

**To order any copy, visit your local Christian bookstore
or go to www.WPHonline.com!**

The Abundant Life Is the Generous Life

Generosity does not come naturally for most of us, yet it is the first economic principle in God's kingdom. Time after time, God's Word instructs us to be generous with what God gives us. This is how we honor God, impact others, and receive a blessing in the process.

In *Give to Live*, veteran pastor Stan Toler inspires and equips Christians to live generously and to trust God with their finances and lives. This timely and practical book includes a full study guide with small-group discussion questions for each chapter. Embrace the abundant life today!

Give to Live: The Freedom of Being Generous with Your Life
ISBN: 978-0-89827-595-7

wesleyan
publishing
house

**Available from your local bookstore or
call WPH Direct: 1.800.493.7539**